T.S.I.T.S.
Things Seen in the Spirit

By Lady Mary Hatter

© Copyright 2016, Lady Mary Hatter

All Rights Reserved.

No part of this book may be reproduced or transmitted in any form or by any means, electronic or mechanical, including photocopying, recording or by any information storage and retrieval system, without the written permission of the Publisher, except where permitted by law.

ISBN: 978-1-60414-902-9

Published by Mary Hatter
Spring, Texas 77373

Cover Design / Creation by Mary Hatter

Unless otherwise noted, all Scripture references are from the King James Version of the Bible. 1972, 1976, 1979, 1983, 1984 1985 Thomas Nelson Inc. Publishers.

Dedication/Acknowledgements

I dedicate this book to my wonderful husband, Andre, who I love dearly. He is my friend, partner, and Pastor.

Also to my daughter, son and granddaughter. Tangeneva L. Wilson, Tristian A. Hatter, and Maranda J. Wilson, I love you. I am so Godly proud of both my children and excited and thankful to God about our first granddaughter from Tangeneva.

To all the wonderful members and partners of Kingdom Minded Church thanks for allowing me to be a part of your lives.

I thank God for Jesus, who saved me and called, chose, and commissioned me to go ye therefore and help build up his Kingdom. To God be the glory, for all the things he has done and yet to do in my life and yours. Thank God for allowing his Spirit to reveal all things to me as I speak his Word as his Spirit gives me the utterance. Thank you.

Table of Contents

Things Seen in the Spirit
Dedication/Acknowledgements iii
Purpose of This Book vii
Introduction ix

Month of January 1
Month of February 3
Month of March 6
Month of April 15
Month of May 27
Month of June 42
Month of July 55
Month of August 66
Month of September 80
Month of October 85
Month of November 93
Month of December 102
Author's Comments 113

Confessions Journal 115
    Introduction 117
    Journal 119

Book of Revelations 145
    Introduction 147
    Divine Disclosures of Best Kept Secrets 149

About the Author 235

Purpose of This Book

1) Printed for a purpose for all to see and read
2) Purpose is for what God wants all people to hear listen and do
3) People lives will change and be better because they know the plans of God
4) Plans that God gives us to followed and receive promotions from him
5) Promotions that only come through God and receive all his promises
6) Promises that God has already set up for you to receive his prosperity
7) Prosperity that gives God pleasure and that's our ultimate goal is to please him

Introduction

I am so amazed! What revelations! This is like something I have never experienced before. God has been speaking to me by His Spirit for some years. I didn't quite understand it at first. I talked to my husband, Pastor A.D. Hatter. I began to tell him what I was hearing and seeing, which was coming to pass immediately. He told me I have the prophetic anointing on my life. God reveals his secret unto his prophets. (See Amos 3:7) Surely the Lord God will do nothing, but he revealeth his secret unto his servants the prophets. I have over ten years of notes in my spiral notebooks. I wrote down these things that God spoke to me, through his Spirit. I heard God say, write this book and he gave me the name also, which is *T.S.I.T.S. Things Seen In The Spirit*.

My prayer is that, people of God who he has called to do his work will hear and listen and do as He says. We must understand and be sure of our calling. (See 2 Peter 1:10) Wherefore the rather, brethren, give diligence to make your calling and election sure; for if ye do these things, ye shall never fail: I pray for the saved that read my book, if not filled with Holy Spirit, will be filled, and with evidence of speaking in tongues; and interpretation also.(see 1 Corinthians 14:13-15)

To the unsaved who read my book, I pray you receive Jesus, as your Lord and Saviour. As tongues are for a sign to those who believe not. (See 1 Corinthians 14:22) also (see Romans 10:9, 13).

I am writing this book to reveal the secrets God wants his people to know. Again hear, listen, and do as God instructs you to do, you will receive his blessings and never fail in doing his work. I pray for your obedience and keeping of Gods commandments and living the life he called, and chose you to live. Extras: Faith Confessions; Words spoken by God through His Spirit, for Kingdom Minded Church and all who will hear and do. Thanks.

MONTH OF JANUARY

January 20
Scripture of the Day: It is written in the prophets and they shall be all taught of God. Every man therefore that hath heard and learned of the Father, cometh unto me. (John 6:45)

January 21
Build your Kingdom first, then bless others, charity starts at home and spreads abroad. Have faith and forgive. You will remember, but the blood of Jesus will help you get past the pain. Once you get past the pain you receive your benefits of having your P.H.D. Pain to *Pleasure*. Hurt to *Holy Spirit*. Devastation to *Devotion*. *This is the Word from God!*

And Jesus answering saith unto them, have faith in God. And when ye stand praying, forgive, if ye have ought against any; that your Father also which is in heaven may forgive you your trespasses. (Mark 11:22, 25)

How much more shall the blood of Christ, who through the eternal spirit offered himself without spot to God, purge your conscience from dead works to serve the living God? (Hebrews 9:14)

January 22
Word for Pastor A.D. and Lady Mary Hatter: You've been faithful and because of your faithfulness it's your time! Everything we have confessed in the Spirit realm is revealed and received in the natural

realm. God speaks harvest I receive it now! Holy Spirit gives revelation I receive it now! Nothing and no one can stop my overflow; I reach and receive now!

God says He'll give you revelations from the Spirit like never before. You can't find what He has to say in a book. God is taking Pastor A.D. and I higher and higher we won't look back or come down. Don't worry about being taken care of by the church. God will always take care of you.

Don't base your decision on what the church can do, base it on what God can do, and what He says do. Continue with the principles being taught through Bishop I.V. Hilliard don't allow anyone to change your direction, even the Baptist Church and its traditions and old ways. Don't settle for less in the hundreds we will reach thousands, if we continue the path we are following and going. Remember (Philippians 3:13-14). Don't be subjected to past traditions, continue on in the faith and principles we are living. God will increase us if we stay on this path.

We'll be stuck with the hundreds and not the thousands if we don't allow Him to increase. One planted one watered but God gives increase. Don't despise the small things. Don't hurry God. He knows your time and will release in His time, everything He has already laid up for you, quickly and suddenly. *This is the Word from God!*

MONTH OF FEBRUARY

February 15

Word for Pastors and Spouses: You're blessed in the city and blessed in the field. You've been faithful over the little and now I'm sending many. This is the birth that I've caused. I'm sending prayer warriors, praisers, prophets and preachers. They shall be like their master but not above their master. Receive them now!

The blood of Jesus covers you in every situation in your life. You shall reap where you have not sown. This is the increase that I've caused, said the Lord. What God put together no man can separate. I give you keys to open doors that were shut and open new doors. Enter in now! Saith the Lord.

The vision shall come to pass now! You shall receive everything and more back that was stolen from you. Your children shall speak in tongues and interpret. They shall have dreams and visions. I'm sending skilled workers, anointed musicians, and singers. Because you've been a blessing to the Kingdom, I'm blessing your house! Saith the Lord. Quickly, suddenly and right now!

What I'm sending you; no man can take away. Receive your wealthy place now! Enjoy the blessings from me. Always remember to be a blessing and remember I have caused this increase. *This is the Word from God!*

February 19

Word from God! Continually: God says, I'm his instrument being used continually by him. He has given me control over my enemies. I must receive the treasures of darkness, continually. Know that I'm the Lord, which calls you by name continually, and I'm God alone. I must continually obey, serve and keep his commandments. Therefore he will continually bless me, that I continually bless others. *And I will give thee the treasures of darkness and hidden riches of secret places that thou mayest know that I, the Lord, which call thee by name am the God of Israel* (Isaiah 45:3)

February 24

I'm Called, Charged, Chosen, Corrected and Completed. Receive your reward. This is the promotion I've caused. The people will see God in this. It's all about him. *This is the Word from God!*

February 25

Scriptures of the Day: Behold I send you forth as sheep in the midst of wolves: be ye therefore wise as serpents and harmless as doves: but beware of men: for they will deliver you up to the councils, and they will scourge you in their synagogues: and ye shall be brought before governors and kings for my sake, for a testimony against them and the Gentiles, but when they deliver you up, take no thought how or what ye shall speak; for it shall be given you in that same hour what ye shall speak. For it is not ye that speak, but the Spirit of your Father which speaketh in you. (Matthew 10:16-20)

Now I beseech you, brethren mark them which cause division and offences contrary to the doctrine which ye have learned; and avoid them. For they that are such serve not our Lord Jesus Christ, but their own belly; and by good words and fair speeches deceive the hearts of the simple. (Romans 16: 17-18)

February 25

Word from God! It's not over until God says it's over. Keep fighting until the victory is won.

February 26

Word for U.P.E. Designs: Your job can't get you the wealth that I'm sending. Meditate on the creative ideas and inventions I've already blessed you with. I'm sending people to help you and customers from everywhere. Your gift is in your mind and hands. Start picturing your designs in your thoughts daily, customers paying you for orders and contracts for Weddings, Church, Residential, and Business. Start giving to the less fortunate. Decorating the shelters and victims of disasters. Give and it shall be given unto you, good measure, pressed down, shaken together, and running over shall men give unto your bosom. The key is giving to the poor. You're blessed to be a blessing. *This is the Word from God!*

As it is written, he hath dispersed a broad: he hath given to the poor: his righteousness remaineth forever. (2 Corinthians 9:9)

MONTH OF MARCH

March 1

Word from God! When things try to get out of control speak out loud. Flesh I check you in the name of Jesus! You profit me nothing! You have no good things! Leave now in Jesus name!

Then saith Jesus unto him, get thee hence Satan for it is written thou shalt worship the Lord thy God and him only shalt thou serve. Then the devil leaveth him and behold angels came and ministered unto him. (Matthew 4:10-11)

March 7

We received a move of God like never before, in our homes and in our hearts. We're good stewards over what God has given us, and we bless when he says bless, and who he wants us to bless. We made the first step last night in blessing the Cyrus family with a bedroom set for the boys. We have received favor before finances. Because you have given to those in need as I have given you, your bedroom set. You activated the blessings of the Lord coming on you and overtaking you. *This is the Word from God!*

March 7

Scripture of the Day: And it shall come to pass, if thou shalt hearken diligently unto the voice of the Lord thy God, to observe and to do all his commandments which I command thee this day, that the Lord thy God will set thee on high above all nations of the earth. And all these blessings shall come on thee, and overtake thee, if thou shalt hearken unto the voice of the Lord thy God.

Blessed shalt thou be in the city, and blessed shalt thou be in the field. The Lord shall open unto thee his good treasure, the heaven to give the rain unto thy land in his season and to bless all the work of thine hand, and thou shalt lend unto many nations, and thou shalt not borrow. And the Lord shall make thee the head, and not the tail; and thou shalt be above only, and thou shalt not be beneath; if that thou hearken unto the commandments of the Lord thy God, which I command thee this day to observe and to do them.(Deuteronomy 28:1-3,12-13)

March 8

God says we must continue to plant the Word of God in our hearts and mind. Be hearers and doers of his Word. We will never hunger nor thirst. We shall receive increase automatically, when we wake up theirs increase, increase when we expect it and when we're not expecting it. Increase is all around us, and it's automatic. Immediately increase is in our house, our barns are filled with plenty. Receive now saith the Lord. *This is the Word from God!*

And he said, so is the Kingdom of God as if a man should cast seed into the ground; And should sleep, and rise night and day, and the seed should spring and grow up he knoweth not how, For the earth bringeth forth fruit of herself, first the blade then the ear, after that the full corn in the ear. But when the fruit is brought forth immediately he putteth in the sickle, because the harvest is come. (Mark 4:26-29)

March 9

God says he has reserved the blessings for me; I must receive my on time reservation of blessings from Him right now! The blessings are on me now! God says He's the greatest, so expect the great. He has pleasure in giving me the Kingdom.

The fire burns everything that's not like Him; now receive all that's of Him. Today is our day to receive the miracles from God. Expect nothing but the best because I can place an order without worrying about how much it costs. There's no limit to God.

Everything I've asked according to His Word, it's done for me now! Everything shall continually be revealed by my Spirit saith the Lord. Believe ye my prophets, so shall ye prosper; there's money in the mouth of the prophet. Receive your money now! Receive your overflow, overtaking of blessings now! I've promised you that all my promises are yes and Amen.

You must say yes and agree with Me for all of My promises saith the Lord. I've poured you out blessings that you have not enough room to receive them. You shall disperse to the poor and those in need and receive the fullness of God now. *This is the Word from God!*

March 10

God says He is King of kings and Lord of lords. It's His Kingdom that has come and His will that's being done; right here on earth as it is in heaven. I have given you the keys to the Kingdom and we unlock every door that He wants us to enter in.

I have created all things and given you headship over them. You speak to mountains; they are removed never to return. Everything that was dead in your life now lives. Your angels work for you; they hearken unto your voice.

Holy Spirit reveals all things to you. God says you know how to follow; now you must lead. If my people, which are called by My name, shall humble themselves, pray, and seek My face and turn from their wicked ways, then will they hear from heaven and I will forgive their sin, and will heal their land.

I've given you Kingdom Minded Church to teach My people My principles, My Word, My ways, and they shall receive of Me and keep My Word and do as I command them this day. When the people receive My Word, you're teaching and apply My Word to their lives, they will receive life-changing experiences, increase blessings, and be rewarded in every area of their lives. They will know you are truly sent by Me. *This is the Word from God!*

The prophet which prophesieth of peace, when the word of the prophet shall come to pass, then shall the prophet be known that the Lord hath truly sent him. (Jeremiah 28:9)

March 17

Words from God! When we sing and praise Him he'll destroy our enemies. When we sing and praise God it brings us Riches, Rest, Reign; *(2 Chronicles 20:22,25,30-31); vs. 22 and when they begin to sing and to praise, the Lord set ambushments against the children of Ammon, Moab, and Mount Se-Ir, which were come against Judah; and they where smitten.* (First: Riches) *vs. 25 and when Je-Hosh-A-Phat and his people came to take away the spoil of them, they found among them in abundance both riches with the dead bodies, and precious jewels, which they stripped off for themselves, more than they could carry away; and they were three days in gathering of the spoil, it was so much.* (Second:Rest) *vs. 30 so the realm of Je-Hosh-A-Phat was quiet; for his God gave him rest round about.* (Third: Reign) *vs. 31 and Je-Hosh-A-Phat reigned over Judah; he was thirty and five years old when he began to reign and he reigned twenty and five years in Jerusalem.*

March 19

Words from God! Souls come, favor comes, and finances come when we praise God. Praising God, and having favour with all the people, and the Lord added to the church daily such as should be saved. (Acts 2:47) Ask of me, and I shall give thee the heathen for thine inheritance and the uttermost parts of the earth for thy possession. (Psalm 2:8)

March 19

God has given me a Faith S.E.M. Card; I have the *Substance* when I *See & Speak* the things that I hope for. I receive the *Evidence & Experience* of the *Eternal* things not seen. The things are *Made, Manifested & Mounted* in my faith. The things I receive are based on my faith in Him, saith the Lord. You must continue to believe what I say shall come to pass, even when I can't see it right now!

What I promised I won't take back. I'm a man of My Word, saith the Lord.

I've already laid the blessings up for you, now you must do your part, in having faith, continue to believe me through hard times, because they're temporary, only for a moment. You shall receive all my promises; if it wasn't so I wouldn't have said it. Stay in faith, live life like you're *Resting, Reigning & Receiving* my promises now. This is your time of manifested, overtaking of blessings. You shall receive, quickly suddenly right now! *This is the Word from God!*

March 22

We must Protect The Anointing: Pray Through Adversities: then we receive the Promises, Triumphs, and Advancements: as well as Promotions and Treasures Always: *This is the Word from God!*

March 22

The Glory Clouds are Moving: our Gifts are clearly manifesting, and my Grace covers many; hear and listen to the Words I speak they give light in dark situations. I have touched your mind. I've given you power and ability to get wealth. Choose life, choose the blessings, receive now, all I've prepared for you, there's no lack in the Kingdom, and no lack in your house.

Everything around you is blessed. Be watchful and pray, guard your heart against foolish conversation, speak good and not evil, edify and build up. People will come with the wrong motives; you must recognize the schemes and tricks of Satan. He comes to rob, steal, kill and destroy your good name, your blessings, your anointing, your gifts and your grace.

I will receive the glory saith the Lord. I've given you *protection*, *promises*, *promotions*, and *provisions*. If you continue in my Word, serve me, obey me, and keep my commandments, you shall not be in want of anything. I shall supply all your need and give you the desires of your heart. *This is the Word from God!*

If ye continue in the faith grounded and settled, and be not moved away from the hope of the gospel, which ye have heard, and which was preached to every creature which is under heaven; where of I Paul am made a minister. Where of I am made a minister, according to the dispensation of God which is given to me for you, to fulfill the Word of God; To whom God would make known what is the riches of the glory of this mystery among the Gentiles, which is Christ in you, the hope of glory. Whom we preach, warning every man and teaching every man in all wisdom; that we may present every man perfect in Christ Jesus. (Colossians 1:23, 25, 27-28).

March 25

Words from God! Stable, Strong, and Secure; I've given you a Kingdom Minded Church because you're stable, strong, and secure. You don't waiver to every doctrine. You know my Words, teach my Words, obey and serve me. You don't bend or break and you are not tossed to and fro. You're fitly joined together and following My principles. You teach sound doctrine.

Because you're walking in love you'll never fail. Love always abounds in you forever. Don't be afraid of what the enemy sends your way. You're in control. You command things, as I've already set before you blessings, not curses. Life and not death.

You're more than conquerors through Christ Jesus. I've given you my son; his blood keeps and cover you in every area of your life. I'm a man of my Word. Be ye also ready for the many blessings to come, right now. Again be ye also ready, my blessings are overtaking you!

Expect the great! Expect the great! *Live, Love, Life,* this is your hour that has come. Because you've obeyed and served me, you're receiving the good of the land. Your house has been made fat. Your barns are filled with plenty. It's your time. Receive now!

March 25

Scriptures of the Day: Surely the Lord God will do nothing, but he revealed his secret unto his servants the prophets. The lion hath roared, who will not fear? The Lord God hath spoken, who can prophesy? (Amos 3:7-8)

For we can't but speak the things which we have seen and heard. (Acts 4:20)

Before I formed thee in the belly I knew thee and before thou camest forth out of the womb I sanctified thee, and I ordained thee a prophet unto the nations. (Jeremiah 1:5)

March 29

Prostitution and Fornication: Sanctified and Holy; God says singles having sex prostitute themselves when they don't have a marriage license. Prostitution for singles is sex without a marriage license. Fornication is filthy, unfavorable sex, and without lovemaking or a marriage license. These two things are related. Singles having sex are not only fornicators but they are prostitutes. Prostitution is for hire and fornication is for free. Singles your body belong to me.

You should be sanctified and holy being in subjection to me. I've given you a clean temple and nothing dirty shall enter in. Single females your body is for the male mate I've prepared to find and marry you, so he receives favor from me. You are dismissing his favor from me, when you give yourselves to him in sexual pleasures without a marriage license. Single males you are causing the singles females to be hidden and not found by their husbands I've prepared for them.

I've created you male and female, blessed you to be fruitful and multiply, replenish the earth, subdue it and have dominion over everything. Don't turn away from what I've created you to be, to do, and to have. You shall turn away from prostitution and fornication and be sanctified and holy. If you choose me, you shall live and not die. So, choose life and not death, choose the blessing and not the curse.

Single males, you shall receive favor like never before. Single females you shall receive love like never before. Receive the mate that

I've prepared for you and receive the blessings like never before. *This is the Word from God!*

Whoso findeth a wife findeth a good thing and obtaineth favor of the Lord. (Proverbs 18:22)

So God created man in his own image, in the image of God created he him, male and female created he them. And God blessed them, and God said unto them, be fruitful and multiply and replenish the earth, and subdue it; and have dominion over the fish of the sea, and over the fowl of the air, and over every living thing that moveth upon the earth. (Genesis 1:27-28)

For this cause God gave them up unto vile affections: for even their women did change the natural use into that which is against nature. And likewise also the men leaving the natural use of the woman, burned in their lust one towards another; men with men working that which is unseemly and , and receiving in themselves that recompense of their error which was not meet. And even as they didn't like to retain God in their knowledge, God gave them over to a reprobate mind, to do these things which are not convenient. (Romans 1:26-28)

March 31

Words from God! Eight Things About Faith; First: Faith Comes; So then faith comes by hearing, and hearing by the Word of God. (Romans 10:17)

Second: Faith is Now. Now faith is the substance of things hoped for, the evidence of things not seen. (Hebrews 11:1)

Third: Faith is Given; For I say through the grace given unto me, to every man that is among you, not to think of himself more highly than he ought to think; but to think sober, according as God hath dealt to every man the measure of faith. (Romans 12:3)

Fourth: Faith is Work; Even so faith, if it hath not works, is dead, being alone. (James 2:17)

Fifth: Faith is Pleasing God. But without faith it is impossible to please him; for he that cometh to God must believe that he is, and that he is a rewarder of them that diligently seek him. (Hebrews 11:6)

Sixth: Faith is Believing; And Jesus answering saith unto them, have faith in God. (Mark 11:22)

Seventh: Faith is Obeying; By faith Abraham, when he was called to go out into a place which he should after receive for an inheritance, obeyed; and he went out not knowing whither he went. (Hebrews 11:8)

Eighth: Faith is Overcoming; By faith they passed through the Red Sea as by dry land: which the Egyptians assaying to do were drowned. (Hebrews 11:29)

MONTH OF APRIL

April 2

You shall receive a Sudden Turn around and Spiritual Transformation. Don't give up, don't lose heart. Pray the people release of the wrong mindset. They are trying to make a blessing and they will miss a blessing. I never lie, I'm a man of my Word and your blessings are final, there's no negotiation, it's done, receive now, saith the Lord.

Again I say as I told you before, don't be afraid of what the enemy sends your way. Don't stop confessing what I've spoken, it's your time, your hour has come, receive now!

You've been faithful over the little now I've made you ruler over many. My Word shall not return void it shall accomplish that which I please and prosper where to I sent it. The people are *released* from the mindset of *rejection;* you shall *remain* the only name in their mind as their Pastor. *This is the Word from God!*

April 4

Prepared Provided Promises: Reassured Ready Reap; Evidence Exactly Everlasting. I've prepared and provided the promises. I've reassured you now get ready to reap. My evidence is exactly what I've said and is everlasting. As I told you before about faith; faith is the substance of the things, I've already prepared, provided, and promised.

You have my Word, now believe and be reassured what I say, and be ye also ready to reap. Just because you've not received yet, don't mean it's not yours. The unseen rides on your faith in me. You must also believe what I have spoken through my prophets.

Begin to praise me early mornings with a loud voice, shout for joy, be glad and continually magnifying me. I receive pleasure in prospering you. Praise gets my attention. When you praise me, souls are added to the Kingdom and prosperity added to your house. Praise me continually all the day long. Use your power of the tongue and the ability to get all that I've promised and reserved for you. *This is the Word from God!*

Now faith is the substance of things hoped for, the evidence of things not seen. (Hebrews 11:1)

And the Levites, of the children of the Ko`Hath-Ites, and of the children of the Kor`-Hites, stood up to praise the Lord God of Israel with a loud voice on high. And they rose early in the morning and went forth into the wilderness of Te-Ko`A: and as they went forth, Je-Hosh`-A-Phat stood and said, hear me, o Judah and ye inhabitants of Jerusalem; believe in the Lord your God, so shall ye be establish; believe his prophets, so shall ye prosper. (2 Chronicles 20:19-20)

Let them shout for joy, and be glad, that favour my righteous cause; yea, let them say continually, Let the Lord be magnified, which hath pleasure in the prosperity of his servant. And my tongue shall speak of thy righteousness and of thy praise all the day long. (Psalm 35:27-28)

I will bless the Lord at all times; his praise shall continually be in my mouth. O magnify the Lord with me, and let us exalt his name together. *(Psalm 34:1, 3) Praising God and having favour with all the people and the Lord added to the church daily such as should be saved.* (Acts 2:47)

Scripture of the Day: *These six things doth the Lord hate; yea seven are abomination unto him. A proud look, a lying tongue, and hands that shed innocent blood, An heart that deviseth wicked imaginations, feet that be swift in running to mischief, A false witness that speaketh lies, and he that soweth discord among brethren.(Proverbs 6:16-19)*

April 5

When people join your church, they should have the right motives. The people I add to the church will be saved and want to be saved. People with the wrong motives except Jesus because they need something from him; money, and things, and not for their salvation, which I give through Jesus Christ and a new life in him. *This is the Word from God!*

April 6

When we hoard our seed it becomes unaffected. Give as I have directed you to give and who I've said give to. You are blessed to be a blessing. My blessings have movement; they don't stay locked up in the prison of your hands. You're blessed with love, peace, kindness, wisdom, knowledge, and understanding.

You have more than enough money in your hands now than ever before. Release the receiver's blessings now. Once you release the receiver's portion you shall receive another overtaking and overflow of my blessings.

I shall continue this process until the day of Jesus Christ. I shall bless you over and over and over again, if you continue in my Word, obey and serve me, then you will make your way prosperous and shall have good success.

This is my pleasure, which I receive in prospering you. We work together in the blessing arena. You do your part and I'll do mine. *This is the Word from God!*

April 7

Words from God! Water, Wait, Worship; Give unto me the glory due my name; Worship me in the beauty of my holiness. My voice is upon the waters, and I'm upon many waters. Powerful is my voice, and full of majesty. I've given strength unto you and blessed you with peace.

Wait on me, be of good courage and I will strengthen your heart. Rest in me, and wait patiently on me. When you wait on me, you'll receive the inheritance of the earth. I give water to those that thirst after me. You receive all things when you fall down and worship me.

Give unto the Lord the glory due his name; worship the Lord in the beauty of his holiness. The voice of the Lord is upon the waters: the God of glory thundereth: the Lord is upon many waters. The Lord will give strength unto his people; he will bless his people with peace. (Psalm 29:2-3, 11)

But they that wait upon the Lord shall renew their strength; they shall mount up on wings as eagles, they shall run and not be weary. And they shall walk, and not faint. (Isaiah 40:31) *Rest in the Lord, and wait patiently for him: fret not thyself because of him who prospereth in his way, because of the man who bringeth wicked devices to pass. For evildoers shall be cut off: but those that wait upon the Lord, they shall inherit the earth.* (Psalm 37:7, 9)

April 7

My L.E.T.T.E.R. to you. *Love Endures Trials Tests Extraordinary Real.* Because you *love* me and have *endured* the *trials* and *tests*, you receive *extraordinary* and *real* rewards and blessings from me now! I give you this L.E.T.T.E.R. of P.R.O.M.I.S.E. *Provision Revelation Overflow Money Increase Security Every Day.* Place this L.E.T.T.E.R. in your heart, because your heart is pure; lift up your heads, o ye gates, and be ye lifted up, ye everlasting doors; and the king of glory shall come in. You've opened up your heart to me; therefore I give you my Spirit forever. When I send souls to you, you shall speak of my *goodness*, my *grace*, and my *glory*. Every soul I send, and you tell of your testimony, and be a witness for me, I will save them. They shall know the truth and the truth shall make them free. *This is the Word from God!*

He that have clean hands, and a pure heart; who hath not lifted up his soul unto vanity, nor sworn deceitfully. Lift up your heads, o ye gates; and be ye lifted up, ye everlasting doors; and the king of glory shall come in. (Psalm 24:4, 7)

And it shall turn to you for a testimony. For I will give you a mouth and wisdom, which all your adversaries shall not be able to gainsay nor resist. (Luke 21:13, 15)

And ye shall know the truth, and the truth shall make you free. (John 8:32)

April 12

God says the lip of truth shall be established forever, but a lying tongue is but for a moment. Lying lips are abomination to me, but he that tells the truth is my delight. Hear my voice my wise son and heareth my instruction, eat good by the fruit of your mouth, keep your mouth and keep your life, if you don't you will be destroyed and brought to shame.

Husbands love your wives as Christ also loved the church, and gave himself for it; men you must love your wives as your own bodies, for if you love your wife you love yourself. Keep your mouth and tongue; you will keep your soul from troubles. Hear instructions, be wise and refuse it not. *This is the Word from God!*

The lip of truth shall be established for ever: but a lying tongue is but for a moment. Lying lips are abomination to the Lord; but they that deal truly are his delight. (Proverbs 12:19, 22)

A wise son heareth his father's instruction; but a scorner heareth not rebuke. A man shall eat good by the fruit of his mouth; but the soul of the transgressors shall eat violence. He that keepeth his mouth keepeth his life: but he that openeth wide his lips shall have destruction. A righteous man hateth lying but a wicked man is loathsome, and cometh to shame. (Proverbs 13:1-3, 5)

Husbands love your wives, even as Christ also loved the church, and gave himself for it; So ought men to love their wives as their own bodies. He that loveth his wife loveth himself. (Ephesians 5:25, 28)

Whoso keepeth his mouth and his tongue keepeth his soul from troubles. (Proverbs 21:23)

Hear instruction, and be wise, and refuse it not. (Proverbs 8:33)

April 13

Station, Serve, Seek, Solid, Secure: Because you seek after right and righteousness and serve me, you are solid, secure and stationed. This place I've given you shall bring long life, riches and wealth to my Kingdom and your house. I'm your Father and you're my child. I will never abandon you nor forget about you. Even in these days of famine you shall be satisfied with everything I've already blessed you with and more.

Continue to use your mouth and your hands to be a blessing and you will continue to receive my blessings. Love my people; feed my sheep, they hunger and thirst after righteousness. Those that are in want shall never go hungry or thirsty, because they want from me. Jesus is the way, the truth, and the life; no one can come to me without going through him first. Use what I've given you.

Angels have keeping power, and charge over you; let them work for you. Holy Spirit reveals all things unto you, he helps you to speak and move as I have said. Again use what I've given you, don't be afraid of the enemy he only has a bark and not a bite. I've made you, and it was without any help from you. I've given you your sword and shield, I've given you protection and my Word, *rest* in me, *receive* of me, *reign* in me. These are the end times, but everlasting times for you. Your latter is greater.

Every seed you've sown has manifested and you receive even where you've not sown. I say this again. I give you reminders to remember me always, I've caused this wealth and people will know it's of me. I do this because we work together in the harvest field.

You are on your own in the land of not enough, because I'm a God of more than enough and plenty. I give you power and ability to get wealth, so always call those things that be not as though they were. I heal all sickness and diseases, call them gone now. All my promises are yes and Amen, so call them to you now, so again I say to you, everything

Things Seen in the Spirit

you need and want is in your mouth, it's in your hands, so reach and receive now. *This is the Word from God!*

But this is that which was spoken by the prophet Joel; And it shall come to pass in the last days, saith God, I will pour out of my Spirit upon all flesh: and your sons and your daughters shall prophesy, and your young men shall see visions, and your old men shall dream dreams:

And on my servants and on my handmaidens I will pour out in those days of my Spirit; and they shall prophesy: And I will shew wonders in heaven above, and signs in the earth beneath; blood, and fire, and vapour of smoke:

This Jesus hath God raised up, whereof we all are witnesses. Therefore being by the right hand of God exalted, and having received of the Father the promise of the Holy Ghost, he hath shed forth this, which ye now see and hear. (Acts 2:16-19, 32-33)

Let your conversation be without covetousness; and be content with such things as ye have for he hath said, I will never leave thee, nor forsake thee. (Hebrews 13:5)

In the last day, that great day of the feast, Jesus stood and cried, saying if any man thirst let him come unto me, and drink. He that believeth on me, as the scripture hath said out of his belly shall flow rivers of living water. (John 7:37-38)

Jesus saith unto him, I am the way, the truth, and the life; no man cometh unto the Father, but by me. (John 14:6)

As it is written I have made thee a father of many nations, before him whom he believed, even God, who quickeneth the dead, and calleth those things which be not as though they were. (Romans 4:17)

For he shall give his angels charge over thee, to keep thee in all thy ways. (Psalm 91:11)

April 14

Asset and Not a Liability; Always Abounding Never in Lack; Anointed and received a New Life; I give you full coverage. You have abundance in every area of your life. I anointed you and you've received a new life. I can use you for my Kingdom. My glory is revealed, my grace I give you, and my gifts I give you.

Your prophesies are unlimited and you speak to unlimited amount of people. There are no limits for me and none for you. There are no secrets to what I can do. Because my secrets are revealed through you, you speak what, when, and where I say speak.

All things are revealed by my Spirit, and I give you my Spirit. Never be afraid or question or wonder if it's me. My Spirit is upon you and I'm not the initiator of confusion, I do things descent and in order and so will you. This is a new life for you and you shall receive until the day of Jesus Christ.

Forget not my sayings, write the vision, make it plain, it shall speak and not lie. You never miss or forget what I speak to you, it's by my Spirit. *This is the Word from God!*

My son, attend to my Words, incline thine ear unto my sayings. Let them not depart from thine eyes; keep them in the midst of thine heart. (Proverbs 4:20-21)

But he that prophesieth speaketh unto men to edification, and exhortation, and comfort. Wherefore tongues are for a sign, not to them that believe, but to them that believe not: but prophesying serveth not for them that believe not, but for them which believe. For God is not the author of confusion, but of peace, as in all churches of the saints. Let all things be done decently and in order. (1 Corinthians 14:3, 22, 33, 40)

Being confident of this very thing, that he which hath begun a good work in you will perform it until the day of Jesus Christ: (Philippians 1:6)

April 14

You shall receive in seasons. Every season come throughout the year. You shall receive all the year long. You have different blessings in each season. Prospering season, increase of souls season, healing and deliverance seasons. This process I continued year after year, which means I continually bless you, over and over again. *This is the Word from God!*

April 17

Render, Reap, Rejoice, Renew, Ready, Ripe; God says render service to him and you'll reap the harvest of his blessings. Rejoice and be exceedingly glad. I've renewed your mind to think things of me and cast down anything that's not of me.

You're ready to do all things as unto me and receive everything thing that's become ripe, which is being brought to full completeness from me. Again, I say to you, thousands shall hear and learn of me and do as I say, because I've given you my Word to speak to them.

Let my Words be in your mouth at all times, meditate day and night. When you open your mouth and speak my Words, I shall give you plenty food to chew on and process, that you'll be full always. *This is the Word from God!*

April 19

Where your heart is, there shall your treasure be also. The answer is in the question. If your heart is in your job, that's where your trust for money is. If your heart is in your business God gave you, which is U.P.E. Designs, that's where your money is. If your heart is for the people, and God's Kingdom, that's where your money is. When you seek after things for my sake or after me, I will give you treasures from heaven.

White fields are ready to harvest, seek after your match and work in the harvest field; receive all the monies for your labour; give me my portion, disperse to those in need, and I shall pour you out blessings you won't have enough room to receive. Your labour in my harvest fields shall not be in vain. You shall reap the harvest of my blessings; you shall receive miracles of things you expected and have not expected. *This is the Word from God!*

But lay up for yourselves treasures in heaven, where neither moth nor rust do corrupt, and where thieves do not break through nor steal: For where your treasure is, there will your heart be also. (Matthew 6:20-21)

Say not ye, there are yet four months, and then cometh the harvest? Behold, I say unto you, lift up your eyes, and look on the fields; for they are white already to harvest. And he that reapeth receiveth wages, and gathereth fruit unto life eternal: that both he that soweth and he that reapeth may rejoice together. And herein is that saying true, one soweth, and another reapeth I sent you to reap that whereon ye bestowed no labour: other men laboured, and ye are entered into their labours. (John 4:35-38)

Bring ye all the tithes into the storehouse, that there may be meat in mine house, and prove me now here-with, saith the Lord of hosts, if I will not open you the windows of heaven, and pour you out a blessing, that there shall not be room enough to receive it. (Malachi 3:10)

April 27

God says, I didn't put you on lay-a-way, to be put on a shelf waiting on someone to make a payment for you. Jesus paid it all for you. Your debt is paid in full. Get up and get out and work while its day because when night comes no man can work. I've given you a straight and narrow path; don't go outside your boundaries.

Work within your parameters. Don't try and do something I've not prepared, placed and position you to do. Your success lies in your hands along with the helpers I've given you. Use what I gave you; call on your angels, Holy Spirit and most importantly Jesus.

The oil is in your hands, touch who and what I say touch. Receive only what I've laid up for you. Your blessings again, are in your mouth, speak what I've reserved for you, before you were in your mother's womb. Receive now all my promises that I've said yes and Amen to!

Don't worry or think about the haters, they're there to strengthen you. When they say you can't or what you're not, I say you can and is. Listen, pay attention, and hear me, my child. I'm your Lord, you obey and serve me and keep my commandments.

I give you power to get wealth, I give you power over the enemy, I give you power to speak to dead situations and they live. Holy Spirit is upon you, and reveals all things that I've spoken to you. Listen carefully don't miss me when I'm speaking, use your gifts I've given you and your helpers. Be ready for the promptings and prophesies of your preparer which is me.

I'm the creator of all things; I did this with the Words of my mouth. I've given you dominion over all things and you must follow my lead and do the same with your mouth. Use only my Words which my Spirit speaks to you, this is the key to your success. Start receiving now, everything that has been stolen, stationed and secured for you. *This is the Word from God!*

And Jesus looking upon them saith, with men it is impossible, but not with God: for with God all things are possible. Then Peter began to say unto him, lo, we have left all and have followed thee. And Jesus answered and said, verily I say unto you, there is no man that hath left house, or brethren, or sisters, or father, or mother, or wife, or children, or lands, for my sake, and the gospel's, But he shall receive an hundredfold now in this time, houses, and brethren, and sisters, and mothers, and children, and lands, with persecutions; and in the world to come eternal life. But many that are first shall be last; and the last first. (Mark 10:27-31)

Then the Word of the Lord came unto me, saying, Before I formed thee in the belly I knew thee; and before thou cameth forth out of the womb I sanctified thee, and I ordained thee a prophet unto the nations. Then said I, oh Lord God! Behold, I cannot speak: for I am a child. But the Lord said unto me, say not, I am a child: for thou shalt go to all that I shall send thee, and whatsoever I command thee thou shalt speak. Be not afraid of their faces: for I am with thee to deliver thee, saith the Lord. Then the Lord put forth his hand, and touched my mouth, and the Lord said unto me, behold, I have put my Words in thy mouth. See, I have this day set thee over the nations and over the kingdoms to root out, and to pull down, and to destroy, and to throw down, to build, and to plant. (Jeremiah 1:4-10)

And God said, let us make man in our image, after our likeness: and let them have dominion over the fish of the sea, and over the fowl of the air, and over the cattle, and over all the earth, and over every creeping thing that creepeth upon the earth. And God blessed them, and God said unto them, be fruitful and multiply, and replenish the earth, and subdue it: and have dominion over the fish of the sea, and over the fowl of the air, and over every living thing that moveth upon the earth. (Genesis 1:26, 28)

MONTH OF MAY

May 1

Not Distracted but Involved; not Disturbed but Enlightened; not Disappointed but Encouraged; don't be distracted by anything or anyone that the devil tries to send your way. This is his trick to try and stop you from doing the work that I've called you to do.

Stay involved and continue in my Word, you'll never fail. Be not disturbed but enlightened. I've lifted you away from the hands of the enemy. If I be lifted up, I'll draw all men unto me. So, don't be disappointed but encouraged. No matter the situation that comes, I've given you life and not death in the power of your tongue, speak my Words, they're good, healthy, and marrow to your bones.

You'll receive the good fruit always. You've received your miracles on this third day and nothing and no one can take what I've given you. Stay steadfast, unmovable, always abounding in my work and Word. Because I've established your goings you can't be stopped. *This is the Word from God!*

And Jesus came and spake unto them, saying. All power is given unto me in heaven and in earth. Go ye therefore, and teach all nations, baptizing them in the name of the father, and of the son, and of the Holy Ghost. Teaching them to observe all things whatsoever I have commanded you: and, lo, I am with you always, even unto the end of the world. A-men. (Matthew 28:18-20)

The fruit of the righteous is a tree of life: and he that winneth souls is wise. (Proverb 11:30)

Death and life are in the power of the tongue and they that love it shall eat the fruit thereof. (Proverb 18:21)

May 4

It's time for you to get moving and start making money and receive your manifestation that I've reserved for you. With your creative ideas and witty inventions you must tap into supernatural abundance now! The blessings are on you now! You've planted your seed; you have my attention. I give you the green light. Now go and get your overflow of money now!

I've prepared a place for U.P.E. Designs. Use your mouth, ask for it, use your hands, receive it and continue to work, you'll receive again, I say, overflow of great paying customers from everywhere. Learn of me, I've touched your mind; nothing is impossible with me. You can do all things through Christ which strengthen you.

When you hear my voice, move; make it happen. Money shall manifest quickly, suddenly right now! It's your time and season of breakthrough favor for Money, Making, Moving, and Manifesting in your life. You've received this favor because the Kingdom is in need. I supply all your need, according to my riches and glory through Christ Jesus.

Now you must supply the Kingdom's need as I've blessed you, to be a blessing. My blessings make you rich and adds no sorry, don't make no excuses for your sudden wealth. You are on display for me, as U.P.E. Designs are on display for you. You've received an overflow of blessings like never before. *This is the Word from God!*

Commit thy works unto the Lord, and thy thoughts shall be established. (Proverbs 16:3) *I can do all things through Christ which strengtheneth me.* (Philippians 4:13)

To everything there is a season, and a time to every purpose under the heaven: (Ecclesiastes 3:1)

The blessing of the Lord, it maketh rich, and he addeth no sorrow with it. (Proverbs 10:22)

May 5
Decide, Determine, Direction, Do, Done: Flashing, Following, Finishing, Feeding, Faith, Flowing, Finding, Facts, Fixed: Working, Walking, Washing, Willing, Wealth: When you *decide* to work for the Kingdom you must be *determined*, you must get *directions* from Holy Spirit, *do* as I say, and it shall be *done* unto you.

There's a great work to be done in my Kingdom. Everything that's needed is *flashing* before you. *Follow* the leader, which is Holy Spirit. You shall *finish* what you start. *Feed* my sheep, have *faith* in knowing that I'm always with you, even unto the end of the earth. The anointing is *flowing* freely in you.

The lost are *finding* their way to the Kingdom because of the *facts* you speak to them. You know the truth and the truth makes you free, and their lives are *fixed*, because of the truth you speak and now they start *working* for the Kingdom.

They're *walking* in my promises. I've *washed* them and cleaned them up from all unrighteousness, because they're *willing* and obedient they shall eat the good of the land. My land is flowing with milk and honey, with many mansions, houses, and land, and plenty of *wealth*. This is my *Process, Procedure*, and *Production* for building up my Kingdom. *This is the Word from God!*

But seek ye first the Kingdom of God, and his righteousness; and all these things shall be added unto you. (Matthew 6:33)

And we know that all things work together for the good of them that love God, to them who are the called according to his purpose. (Romans 8:28)

But be ye doers of the Word and not hearers only, deceiving your own selves. (James 1:22)

There is therefore now no condemnation to them which are in Christ Jesus, who walk not after the flesh, but after the Spirit. For the law of the Spirit of life in Christ Jesus hath made me free from the law of sin and death. (Romans 8:1-2)

May 5

Connected, Commissioned, Conference, Crying, Calling, Compassion, and Commandment; People are coming together for the wrong reasons, they're getting together for money, loneliness, sexual pleasures and everything that I've not *connected, commissioned, conference* them together for. Your personal lives are all messed up, because you've chosen to lay me aside. You trust and please yourselves. You believe you can think things through and figure out what to do, once you've satisfied the flesh.

They're *crying* and *calling* for me, but won't hear wisdom, and they won't hear my Word. Wisdom is speaking to them but they incline not an ear. I can only work with those that want and choose to work with me.

Make the choice, hear me; I shall have *compassion* on you, only if you keep my *commandments*. Just like you need me, I need you to want and receive me. I shall rebuke the devourer for your sakes. Come unto me all who labor and are heavy-laden and I'll give you rest. There's rest for the weary, wounded, weeping, and wondering in this world.

Don't seek to satisfy your flesh, seek to satisfy your Spirit, your soul, and Saviour. Choose the best life, which is what I have for you. When you choose me, Holy Spirit shall teach you my ways. You shall receive power; you shall be more than conquerors through Christ Jesus. Receive the finer things in life be happy, don't accept nothing but the best. *This is the Word from God!*

He taught me also, and said unto me; let thine heart retain my Words: keep my commandments, and live. Hear, O my son, and receive my sayings: and the years of thy life shall be many. Take fast hold of instruction: let her not go: keep her; for she is thy life. (Proverbs 4: 4, 10, 13)

Come unto me, all ye that labour and are heavy laden and I will give you rest. Take my yoke upon you, and learn of me; for I am meek and lowly in heart: and ye shall find rest unto your souls. For my yoke is easy, and my burden is light. (Matthew 11:28-30)

But ye shall receive power, after that the Holy Ghost is come upon you: and ye shall be witnesses unto me both in Jerusalem, and in all Judea'- and in Sa-ma'-ri-a, and unto the uttermost part of the earth. (Acts 1:8)

May 9

Team: Sound, Saturated, Souls, Saved, Strong, and Supernatural; I've given you a team that hears and listens to the sound of my voice, the trumpet sound, and the sound of abundance of rain. Souls are saved; because you are saturated and strong in my Word, and I'll supernaturally give you increase in the Kingdom and your house.

You're a survivor; your suffering was for my sake. Because you've responded to the sound, you can receive the abundance of souls saved, continue to be saturated in my Word, strong in the Lord, and supernaturally increased in your house. People will begin to honor you, and bless you in the Kingdom, in your family, and even the world will give to you for my sake. I never go back on my promises or my Word.

What I've spoken has come to pass now! Receive your rewards now! It's all good, and it's all God. *This is the Word from God!*

My sheep hear my voice, and I know them, and they follow me: (John 10:27)

Then they that gladly received his Word were baptized, and the same day there were added unto them about three thousand souls. (Acts 2:41) *For it is better, if the will of God be so, that ye suffer for well doing than for evil doing.* (1 Peter 3:1)

And he that overcometh, and keepeth my works unto the end, to him will I give power over the nations. (Revelation 2:26)

For the scripture saith, thou shalt not muzzle the ox that treadeth out the corn. And, the labourer is worthy of his reward. (1 Timothy 5:18)

For this cause pay ye tribute also; for they are God's minister's attending continually upon this very thing. Render therefore to all their dues; tribute to whom tribute is due; custom to whom custom, fear to whom fear; honour to whom honour. (Romans 13:6-7)

May 10

Calm, Created, Clothe, Clear, Cash, Cease, Camp, Clap, Conquer, Cover; I give you peace in the midst of the storm. I've created you and clothe you. It's clear you must stay calm as the winds continue to blow and beat upon your house. I give you the cash that's needed to fund my Kingdom and your house. Cease from frustration, fear and foolishness.

I'm sending you into the enemy's camp, don't worry, you're my warrior, you're covered by the blood of Jesus. Clap your hands and praise me for I send the harvest of souls. You're more than conquerors through Christ Jesus. Be ye also ready for the harvest. *This is the Word from God!*

May 11

Keeper, Kindness, Kinship, Kite; I'm a keeper of your soul; I give you my kindness, and my kinship. You're like minded one to another; you're my sheep in my pasture. I speak these words to you, and you incline an ear to hear, listen, and do as I say.

Because you're my sheep you know my voice and obey me and not the stranger. Listen carefully to the Words I speak now. I've made you like a kite. I put you together, and you need me to fly. I use the string and strong wind of my Word to carry you in all directions; from the north, south, east, and the west; as long as I'm handling and holding the string, you shall move higher and higher; there's no coming down unless you get separated from the string, which is your strength that's in me.

If you let go of the string, and come down, then my wind and my Word can't carry you in the directions that I've prepared and need you to go. Don't separate yourself from the string, which is your strength and security. Remember, I'm the one that put you together from the beginning. I spoke my Words, I fitly joined you together and I breathe the breath of life into you.

Just like you're the kite and I'm the string; you need the wind of my Word, to take you higher and higher and receive every place that's already prepared, and provided for you. I will never allow you to get stopped by tree branches above and bushes below. Nothing in the sky and nothing on the ground shall stop you as long as I'm the leader and you're the follower.

Again, continue to stay connected, communicating, and obeying my commandments, you'll never be lead in the wrong direction. *This is the Word from God!*

May 12

You're just like trees. They're planted by the rivers of waters. They're positioned and placed by many waters. I've given you more than enough to survive. My Word says you're planted in the house of the Lord, you obey and serve me, and you receive overflowing and overtaking of my blessings. Harvest is plenteous and I've chosen you in particular and you are my peculiar people; just as you chose a particular tree to plant. This tree brings harvest of fruits and they remain. Trees need watering and you need my Word.

Trees are planted by you and my Word is planted in you. As trees are rooted in the ground and can only be removed if you cut them down, my Word in you abides always unless you choose not to receive them. This comparison brings clarity to all who listens. The branches on trees are necessary for growth as the team, I've prepared for you are necessary for growth. As you plant different types of trees, I allow you to reach all types of people.

There's no racial or financial boundaries. You shall reach the good, the evil and the broken. Branches grow up and out, the north, south, east and west directions. People are coming from the north, south, east and west to be a part of your ministry. Continue to meditate daily and you will continue to be like the trees planted by the rivers of waters, bringing forth fruit in your season, which is now; your leaf won't go bad and everything you do shall prosper now! *This is the Word from God!*

Blessed is the man that walketh not in the counsel of the ungodly, nor standeth in the way of sinners, nor sitteth in the seat of the scornful. But his delight is in the law of the Lord; and in his law doth he meditate day and night. And he shall be like a tree planted by the rivers of water, that bringeth forth his fruit in his season; his leaf also shall not wither, and whatsoever he doeth shall prosper. (Psalm 1:1-3)

I am the vine, ye are the branches; he that abideth in me, and I in him, the same bringeth forth much fruit for without me ye can do nothing. If ye abide in me and my Words abide in you ye shall ask what ye will, and it shall be done unto you. Ye have not chosen me, but I have chosen you, and ordained you, that ye should go and bring forth fruit, and that your fruit should remain; that whatsoever ye shall ask of the father in my name, he may give it you. (John 15:5, 7, 16)

May 17

Temptation, Test, Trial, Trap, Tell, Trick, Triumph, Testimony, Travail, Treasure; Don't listen to the enemy, you're in control. There's no temptation, no test, no trial that the enemy can trap and trick you and tell you that you can't triumph over. You shall travail over the enemy and have a testimony and receive my treasures in this earthen vessel.

Use what only I can provide. Satan can't provide good, he's not in control of good, only evil. You're in control. I've given you the power, and good of the land. Satan only receives from you, what you give him. He can't take what I've given you. You have power and dominion over everything on this earth, including him. Use what I've given you from the beginning and you'll survive, have security, and safety until the end.

Satan is like an evil dog. He feeds off the bones and food you give him, and whatever he finds. He chews on your good furniture and things you possess, and have paid for. He bites the young, old, rich, and poor. He sneaks and sniffs on you before he attacks and kills you.

I've given you the tools to use to protect yourselves. You have my sword and shield, which is your faith in my Word. Demons tremble at the name of Jesus. When you call on the name of Jesus, everything you want, and I want for you, shall happen, and you shall have. There's no failure in me. You can't lose, if you choose and use what I've given you. *This is the Word from God!*

There hath no temptation taken you but such as is common to man: but God is faithful, who will not suffer you to be tempted above that ye are able; but will with the temptation also, make a way to escape, that ye maybe able to bear it. (1 Corinthians 10:13)

For in the time of trouble he shall hide me in his pavilion: in the secret of his tabernacle shall he hide me; he shall set me up upon a rock. (Psalm 27:5)

The thief cometh not, but for to steal, and to kill, and to destroy; I am come that they might have life, and that they might have it more abundantly. (John 10:10)

Delight thyself also in the Lord; and he shall give thee the desires of thine heart. (Psalm 37:4)

May 22

As I look outside my window of the Hilton Hotel on Nasa Rd. Houston, TX, I see this large never ending body of water, different types of birds flying over and landing in water, jet skis, boats, board walk across the water, seating with umbrella over, information booth, markers in the water, houses, businesses, cars, condos, and roads; all surrounding this large body of water.

God says, as I've given the birds free range to fly freely over the water and land in the water, so shall I give you blessings to rise as high as you want to go and enjoy the landing on safe and comfortable waters. This water has a boardwalk that takes you safely across, you have seating areas and enjoyment of jet skis. I give you these things for your pleasure.

As you see the markers there, they are for the blessings and boundaries that I set for you. If you stay within my boundaries, there are no limits to your blessings. As you see the things surrounding the waters and the never ending waters, this is what I've prepared for you.

As I've set you in your prepared place and position, and you obey and follow me, you receive the growth of the things surrounding you. The houses, businesses, and cars. The earth is mine and the fullness thereof and they that dwell there in; so shall you dwell in my land and be fed. I've given you the finer things in life, so enjoy, be happy, don't make excuses for my blessings, what I give, no one can take away.

My blessings make you rich and adds no sorrow. Don't pay attention to the naysayers, evil speaking, and don't worry about your good being spoken evil of. Remember I gave you keys to the Kingdom and blessings in your house. Every door, I open shall never be closed, and every door I shut shall never be opened. I give you permission to enter in my open doors, and you must not open any doors that I've shut.

As you continue to look out into the water, see the evidence of your faith, this is only the beginning of what's prepared and promised to you. Be encouraged your breakthrough favour is here. Receive now! Step out even though you don't know what or where to step on to. When you move, I move just like that. *This is the Word from God!*

May 24

Remember I'm the one that made you, and breathe the breath of life into you. I called you, I chose you, and I commissioned you, and gave you control. Don't forget my Words, and my work. I begun this work in you and shall complete it, until the day of my son's coming.

Your burdens are destroyed, and yokes are removed, by my power. This power I've given you. Your faith isn't in man. Don't worry about the things that are against you. I will never leave you nor forsake you.

Come, as I told Peter. Keep your eyes on me, as my eyes are on you. My love never fails. You are in the safety of my arms. No one knows, or can see the things, that I've prepared for and promised you.

All these things are revealed by my Spirit, even from the beginning. You've demonstrated your love for me and my people. I've given you a foundation, and your work shall be made manifest. Don't ever be discouraged.

Nothing I've given you shall be taken away, because Satan is waiting to receive it. Remember you're still blessed even in the storm. Continue to keep your eyes on me, and theirs safe landing. Receive your reward now. *This is the Word from God!*

Things Seen in the Spirit

That your faith should not stand in the wisdom of men, but in the power of God. But as it is written, eye hath not seen, nor ear heard, neither have entered into the heart of man, the things which God hath prepared for them that love him. But God hath revealed them unto us by his Spirit, for the Spirit searcheth all things, yea, and the deep things of God. For other foundation can no man lay than that is laid, which is Jesus Christ Now if any man build upon this foundation gold, silver, precious stones, wood, hay, stubble; Every man's work shall be made manifest; If any man's work abide which he hath built thereupon, he shall receive a reward.(1 Corinthians 3:11-14)

May 25

Dominion, Deliverance, and Do. Pay attention to the words of David. He praised, he repented, he had patience, he cried out to me, he loved me, and he had faith in me. I gave him dominion over his enemies; I delivered him from the heathen.

Do as I say, it shall come to pass. Just like David did so shall you. Cry out to me, I will hear and answer you. Have patience and praise me in your waiting. Have faith in me. I've given you dominion and deliverance over your enemies. You have everything that I've already provided for you. Speak to me and your situations. Don't be afraid, I have your back, believe and you shall receive. *This is the Word from God!*

Hear me when I call, O God of my righteousness: thou hast enlarged me when I was in distress; have mercy upon me, and hear my prayer. (Psalm 4:1)

Give ear to my words, O Lord, consider my meditation. My voice shalt thou hear in the morning, O Lord; in the morning will I direct my prayer unto thee, and will look up. For thou, Lord. Wilt bless the righteous; with favour wilt thou compass as with a shield. (Psalm 5: 1, 3, 12)

O Lord my God, in thee do I put my trust: save me from all them that persecute me, and deliver me. (Psalm 7:1)

Preserve me, O God: for in thee do I put my trust. (Psalm 16:1)

Hear the right, O Lord, attend unto my cry, give ear unto my prayer that goeth not out of feigned lips.(Psalm 17:1)

Thou hast delivered me from the strivings of the people; and thou hast made me the head of the heathen: a people whom I have not known shall serve me. It is God that avengeth me, and subdueth the people under me. He delivereth me from mine enemies: yea, thou liftest me up above those that rise up against me: thou hast delivered me from the violent man. Therefore will I give thanks unto thee, O Lord, among the heathen, and sing praises unto thy name. Great deliverance giveth he to his king: and sheweth mercy to his anointed, to David, and to his seed forevermore. (Psalm 18:43, 47-50)

May 25

Words from God! My voice shalt thou hear in the morning oh God; in the morning I will direct my prayer to thee and will look up. Lead me oh Lord in thy righteousness, because of mine enemies. Let not thy enemies triumph over me. Let me not be ashamed. Preserve me oh God, in thee do I put my trust. In Jesus name amen.

May 26

I'm the bread of life. It's I that feed you, clothe you, given you your mind, to think the things that's true, honest, just, pure, lovely, and of good report. Don't ever go a day without speaking to and serving me. I'm the living Word, there's no death or darkness in me.

I'm your heavenly Father that gave you your earthly father that provided the seed which gave you life. Just like the seed gave you life, my Word gives you life in the Spiritual realm. You must never stop hearing and listening to me. You must continually pray and praise me, that you receive power to do all things as unto me.

Don't allow people and problems to push you away from me. People and problems will come against you, but they won't last. My Word brings no worry, no weeping, no wondering, and no weariness. Lift up your heads my children. Remember you belong to me. You have everything I've given you from the beginning.

Don't be upset with the little right now, be patience, be prepared, and be productive. I shall produce to you in due season. This is your season, this is your time, and this is it. Just hold fast to my Word, continue to obey and serve me, and keep my Words in your heart.

Ride out the process, for it must come before the promotion. Remember I do things descent and in order. If I gave you the promotion before the process you wouldn't know how to keep the everlasting promotion.

Everything I bless you with is long term, never ending. My blessings are not rented; they're released. I won't take them back, they belong to you.

Never plant your seed in the wrong soil, because the harvest won't come. Remember, I bless you to be a blessing, and this process repeats itself. If your seed is planted in the wrong soil this stops the process of my promotions. Always be lead by my Spirit, because it's by my Spirit, that all things are revealed unto you. Work the process, watch for your promotion, it's here. *This is the Word from God!*

May 27

Watch what you say, in the good times as well as the bad times. My eyes and ears are upon you. Use your mouth for edifying and building up. Let your conversation be seasoned with salt, bringing grace to the hearers, not condemning.

I gave you power in your tongue, to speak life and not death. You shall reap what you sow. Reap the blessings not the curses. Let no filthy corrupt conversation come out of your mouth. Your tongue is as choice silver. Keep your mouth and keep your life.

Perverseness of the tongue therein is a breach in the Spirit. When you keep your mouth and tongue, your soul is kept from troubles. I give you wisdom to lay up knowledge, so make sure your mouth isn't foolish or near destruction.

Don't allow my Word to slip from you at anytime. You have heard of me, learn of me, keep my Words in your heart always and I shall keep you in perfect peace, when your mind is stayed on me. This is the peace that surpasseth all understanding. So in all your getting make sure you get and understanding.

This is the Word from God!

Therefore we ought to give the more earnest heed to the things which we have heard, lest at any time we should let them slip. (Hebrews 2:1)

He taught me also, and said unto me, let thine heart retain my Words: keep my commandments, and live. (Proverbs 4: 4)

May 30

Twenty-eight days until supernatural breakthrough favor! Praise God! Hold on, hang in there, help is here! As you heard my word on the twenty-eighth day of May, Two Thousand and Eleven, at the Prayer Breakfast, which was spoken, you shall receive your supernatural breakthrough favor in thirty days.

All court cases are canceled against you, car loans, and mortgage loans. These loans are erased from the system. They won't be able to find any evidence of your loans existing, completely removed. Don't think about what you need, I know what you need and will supply it.

Continue to seek first my Kingdom and my righteousness and I shall add all things unto you. Make sure you check the company that you keep. Don't listen to foolish speaking, negative speaking, even if it comes from people you love.

Friends bring freedom, fairness, and fun, not draining, drama, and discouragement through their conversations. Don't even hear them. Where I'm taking you, is far beyond their reach. The conversation they're bringing isn't what's really going on.

The enemy is trying to clog your mind and heart with their foolishness, so you don't see where God has already prepared, purposed, processed, and promoted you for. You have twenty-eight days left in this process, so watch what you say, and you shall see what I see and have sanction, and saved you for.

Your seeds have been planted in the right soil. They have been made manifest in your life now, for such a time as this. Believe my prophets, so shall you prosper. *This is the Word from God!*

But now I have written unto you not to keep company, if any man that is called a brother be a fornicator, or covetous, or an idolater, or a railer, or a drunkard, or an extortioner; with such an one no not to eat. But them that are without God judgeth. Therefore put away from among yourselves that wicked person. (1 Corinthians 5:11, 13)

May 31

My joy is your strength and my joy is full. Be strong in me and in the power of my might. Just like weights builds up your natural man, my Word builds up your Spirit man. What you do for one you must do for the other.

I give water to the natural man, and wisdom to the Spirit man. I give the natural man food, favor, and finance because of his faith in the Spirit man. I've turned your dark and void situations into light, and victorious situations. In the beginning when the earth was void and dark, my Words spoken brought light. Even in your present and future situations that look dark and void, you must speak my Word to bring light and victories.

You have dominion over all things including dark and void situations. This means you always win and there is no losing in you. There's no such thing as win some lose some. With me all things are possible to those who believe. Nothing is impossible with me. Fight the good fight of faith, I shall bring it to pass, have faith in me. Use what you got.

You have angels, call and commission them to work, they're waiting, and they hearken unto your voice. Call on the name of Jesus; everything happens for you when you call him. Call on Holy Spirit he leads, guides, teaches, reveals, and helps you to remember everything I have spoken. I've given you all the help you need again, with all this help you can't lose. You're a winner. Use what you got. *This is the Word from God!*

MONTH OF JUNE

June 1

Atmosphere, Access, Anointing, Awesome; Presence, Partaking, Power: The atmosphere, accesses the anointing and awesome presence and partaking of the power that only comes from me. Make sure your atmosphere is right. Check the senders. The people or person that's sending to you and bringing to you. If it's not sent by me, make sure you return to sender. See if the package has my glory, my grace, and my gift.

All good and perfect gift comes from me. Is this package solid or shaky? You are built on a solid foundation, don't allow anyone to shift or shake you off of what I've placed and positioned you on. Is this package damaged or destroyed? Don't allow anyone to damage or destroy what I've built up. You're not destroyed, but raised up by my power.

Is this package labeled with a red tag, *hazardous*, infected needles? Don't accept anyone or anything that's infected with viruses. These viruses and people come to kill you. Be careful and cautious of the senders, these people can bring you life or they can bring you death. I've come to bring you life and life more abundantly.

Is this package sealed, secure, steady, strong, and beautifully wrapped? The senders of this package was commissioned by me. I've placed on their heart what to send you. This perfect gift receive it now! *This is the Word from God!*

June 2

Word for Lady Mary: Demons tremble at the name of Jesus. People are healed when you call on the name of Jesus. I give you power to lay hands on the sick and they be healed. People will try and stop you from believing in me and doing my work.

When you are among the false prophets and teachers, recognize who they are, call on the name of Jesus. They will try to stop you and lock you up. They will try to keep people locked in and believing their doctrine and believing in them.

You must help those that are bound and locked up and believing in man, not me. When you are in the midst of these people, the ones that are bound and locked up by false doctrines and teachings, you must lay hands on them and speak in the name of Jesus. Immediately they shall be changed to my way. Even the false prophets and teachers will receive their healing in the name of Jesus.

People are released and set free in the name of Jesus. Theirs power in the name of Jesus. You have been anointed, with the money cometh anointing, by the laying on of hands, from Dr. Leroy Thompson.

The money cometh anointing is on you. Speak money cometh to me now! I'll never be broke another day in my life! I have more money in my hands than I've had in a long, long, long time. (Bishop I.V. Hilliard) Speak these words daily, even after the manifestation comes. Speak in the name of Jesus after you say these words. Everything comes when you speak in the name of Jesus.

Again, I give you revelations like never before. Hear, listen and do as I say at all times, only touch who I say touch. Don't allow anyone to try and take advantage and use you for your gift. When you're flowing in the anointing and laying hands and speaking in the name of Jesus, not only are the bounded set free, the false prophet's move out your way.

Everyone you touch receives freedom and a new life in Christ Jesus. Receive of me now; you're ready, use your power, of laying hands, in the name of Jesus. *This is the Word from God!*

That at the name of Jesus every knee should bow, of things in heaven, and things in earth, and things under the earth; And that every tongue should confess that Jesus Christ is Lord, to the glory of God the father. (Philippians 2:10-11)

And Jesus answered and said unto him, what wilt thou that I should do unto thee? The blind man said unto him, Lord, that I might receive my sight. And Jesus said unto him, go thy way, thy faith hath made the whole, and immediately he received his sight, and followed Jesus in the way. And whatsoever ye do in Word or deed, do all in the name of the Lord Jesus, giving thanks to God and the father by him. (Colossians 3:17)

Take my brethren, the prophets, who have spoken in the name of the Lord, for an example of suffering affliction, and of patience. (James 5:10)

But go rather to the lost sheep of the house of Israel. Heal the sick, cleanse the lepers, raise the dead, cast out devils; freely ye have received, freely give. (Matthew 10:6, 8)

Let no man deceive you by any means; for that day shall not come except come a falling away first, and that man of sin be revealed, the son of perdition. Who opposeth and exaltath himself above all that is called God or that is worshipped; so that he as God sitteth in the temple of God, shewing himself that he is God. (2 Thessalonians 2:3-4)

Now we command you, brethren, in the name of our Lord Jesus Christ that ye withdraw yourselves from every brother that walketh disorderly, and not after the tradition which he received of us. (2 Thessalonians 3:6)

And Jesus answered and said unto them, take heed that no man deceive you. For many shall come in my name, saying, I am Christ; and shall deceive many. And many false prophets shall rise, and shall deceive many. Then if any man shall say unto you, lo, here is Christ, or there; believe it not. For there shall arise false Christ's, and false prophets, and shall shew great signs and wonders, insomuch that, if it were possible, they shall deceive the very elect. Behold, I have told you before. (Matthew 24: 4-5, 11, 23-25)

June 6

Seek, Sovereign, Saviour, Surround, Surrender, Sight, and Soul, Satisfied; Seek after me, while I might be found. When you seek after me, you find everything that was lost or hidden in your life. I'm the sovereign God that gave you my son and saviour which is Jesus Christ.

Always surrender yourselves to him and surround yourselves with the people I've sent through him. I've given you sight to see things of me, that's by my Spirit, and your soul shall be satisfied. Never forget where you come from.

It's all about me and that I've chosen you to help my people. They will see my goodness, greatness and glory that's revealed in you. You were poor and now you're rich. This wealth only comes from me. You have what you need to build my Kingdom and your house. I've already provided for you in the beginning.

Always remember what was in the beginning was void, and dark which I spoke light. As I spoke, so shall you. You were poor and in lack, now you're rich as you speak now. Again, I say to you every dark and void situation in your life is full and has light. You have more in life to give and to bless my people; live your life.

You have my love, my peace, and my joy. Make it all full because I've filled your barns with plenty. *This is the Word from God!*

June 7

We are in our season of receiving. Everything that's needed and wanted in your house is yours now, receive now! Saith the Lord. You've come back to me in a mighty way. You've corrected the wrong in your life. You're living in agreement with one another, loving each other, praying and studying my Word together.

Because you heard my voice, obeying, serving and listening to me, I give you everything you need and desire, because your desires are my desired for you, I'm so glad to finally release, restore and replace what you allowed to be stolen from you. Receive all of my blessings, don't be picky, don't think all of these blessings couldn't be for you, they are.

You've earned your overflow and overtaking of blessings. Don't let anyone trick or talk you out of your blessings. I'll tell you who to disperse them to. Just because it looks like a desperate situation to you don't mean I need you to help me, in the dispersing process. Never listen to yourself, trust my Spirit, he shall reveal all things to you.

It's very important that you work the distribution process correctly this determines the direction, promotion and promises; I shall continue to proceed and provide you with. Pay close attention to me. Rely on my Spirit always; you'll never miss what I'm saying. Enjoy your portion; don't hold back my portion, because my portion is critical to your receiving and enjoying more and more of your portion.

Again I say, you're blessed over and over again. Remember in the beginning, I created, called, chose and charged you. By my Words spoken, I created and called you out of darkness into my light. I chose you; you didn't choose me. I charged you to be fruitful and multiply, replenish the earth and subdue it.

Everything on this earth including you moves at my command. So everything including money moves at your command. Listen to the voice of Holy Spirit, do as he commands, and you'll never fail. *This is the Word from God!*

June 8

Praise me at another level that you've never praised me before and I'll give you blessings that you've never received before. I've given you the extraordinary, exceeding and abundantly, above all that you can ask or think. It's in your praise. Walk around the wall of your life, shout and praise me, troubles shall fall down flat.

Don't stop praising me and glorifying me. I inhabit your praise, I respond to your praise with great rewards. I love when you praise me, demons tremble when you praise me, supernatural increase come when you praise me, supernatural debt cancelation comes when you praise me, and increase for the Kingdom comes when you praise me.

Cancellation of all cases that's against you come when you praise me. Cases of lawsuits, criminal and civil cases, all cancelled, because you praise me. Praise me with a loud and great shout. Don't stop or forget to continue praising in spite of the wall against you. This is your process of my provisions and promotions I give to you. *This is the Word from God!*

Then I told them of the hand of my God which was good upon me; as also the king's words that he had spoken unto me. And they said, let us rise up and build. So they strengthened their hands for this good work. (Nehemiah 2:18)

So built we the wall; and all the wall was joined together unto the half thereof: for the people had a mind to work. (Nehemiah 4:6)

And it shall come to pass, that when they make a long blast with the ram's horn, and when ye hear the sound of the trumpet, all the people shall shout with a great shout; and the wall of the city shall fall down flat, and the people shall ascend up every man straight before him. And it came to pass at the seventh time, when the priests blew with the trumpets, Joshua said unto the people, shout; for the Lord hath given you the city. So when the people shouted when priests blew with the trumpets; and it came to pass, when they heard the sound of the trumpet, and the people shouted with a great shout, that the wall fell down flat, so that the people went up into the city, every man straight before him, and they took the city. (Joshua 6:5,16,20)

June 10

You must continue to die daily. Jesus died that you might live. You must die to sin and live righteous. You must be crucified with Christ and allow him to live in you. This life you now live in the flesh, live it by faith of my son, who loved you so, that he gave his life for you.

For all have sinned and come short of my glory; there is no condemnation to you if you are in Christ Jesus, walking not after the flesh, but after my Spirit. For by the Spirit of life in Christ Jesus, you are already free from sin and death. Don't allow your sin and iniquities to turn away and withhold your reserved and appointed weeks of harvest. The wages of sin is death, but my gift God is eternal life through Jesus Christ, your Lord. *This is the Word from God!*

I am crucified with Christ nevertheless I live, yet not I, but Christ lived in me; and the life which I now live in the flesh I live by the faith of the son of God, who loved me, and gave himself for me. (Galatians 2:20)

For all have sinned, and come short of the glory of God; (Romans 3:23)

There is therefore now no condemnation to them which are in Christ Jesus, who walk not after the flesh, but after the Spirit. For the law of the Spirit of life in Christ Jesus hath made me free from the law of sin and death. (Romans 8: 1-2)

For if we have been planted together in the likeness of his death, we shall be also in the likeness of his resurrection: knowing this, that our old man is crucified with him, that the body do sin might be destroyed, that henceforth we should not serve sin. (Romans 6:5-6)

June 12

You're like a person at a gun range. You set up with head and earplugs to block out noise, you have a gun for practice and you concentrate on hitting your target. Just like this person at the gun range, you have your tools, and I've equipped you with what's needed to hit the mark. You must press toward the mark, for the prize of the high calling of me in Jesus Christ.

Don't allow anyone or anything to distract you and don't be afraid to shoot for what I've already placed in your reach. Give me your best shot and I will allow you to hit it. Whatever it is.

You're ready to soar, you have your wings, you're not a caterpillar anymore, you're a butterfly. You're fearfully and wonderfully made. Get up from your crawling state and fly. Remember once you've been changed from caterpillar to butterfly you can't return back to a caterpillar. You have your wings; let them take you higher and higher through my son.

Just like the caterpillar is the beginning of a butterfly, you were once a baby and learned to walk and talk and became an adult. I've taken the butterfly through its process and I've taken you through yours. When the butterfly is trapped in your hands, you smash it and it dies.

Don't allow the tricks and schemes of people to trap you and kill you. Be watchful of your fly zone. Know your area and who's leading you to that area. Listen to my Spirit and you'll always have safe travels and landing.

Where there is calmness there's no chaos, where there's silence, there's no shouting. I give you my peace, learn, listen and do. *This is the Word from God!*

I press toward the mark for the prize of the high calling of God in Christ Jesus. (Philippians 3:14)

And the peace of God, which passeth all understanding, shall keep your hearts and minds through Christ Jesus. Those things which you have both learned, and received, and heard, and seen in me, do: and the God of peace shall be with you. (Philippians 4:7, 9)

June 16

I've given you a bridge. This bridge allows you to go to the other side. It covers the water underneath. This bridge gives you protection from everything underneath that could hurt you. It's your safety net. This bridge is not only your cross over, but your connection. This bridge connects you with other travelers that you must meet along the way that will help you get to the other side.

These are the travelers that I connected you with. They will bless you and you'll bless them, and because of the connection my Kingdom is blessed; this is why I connected you with them. What I've allowed to be connected no one can break that connection.

Don't listen to the naysayers and be disconnected from the travelers. Naysayers come to give you wrong directions to throw you off your going to the other side. They're sent by the enemy because he knows what's on the other side. With these connected travelers, my Kingdom and your houses shall be stronger than ever.

Satan's kingdom has fallen down flat. He wants to use anyone he can to help build it back up. Don't be tricked out of your destiny. I give you this bridge most importantly for your security, and for the connected travelers that I've assigned to help you.

If you allow Satan to block the connection or disconnect what I've already set in order for you; you won't receive your other side breakthrough of blessings, for the Kingdom and your house. Allow Holy Spirit to reveal your connected travelers and you'll never be sent in the wrong direction.

You've fasted and prayed for this other side. It's yours now. I gave you these connected travelers as an added bonus. You need them and they need you. They've fasted and prayed also. I've completed this connection for your sakes and mine. My kingdom is at hand. I've prepared the people and place, and now you are in position for promotion. On the other side you have free range to operate in your gifts I've given you. Miracles shall take place on the other side.

Laying on of hands and healing, especially supernatural increase and debt cancellation shall take place on the other side; deliverance immediately shall take place; demons have no authority, they flee immediately on the other side. Every connected traveler and you shall operate in their assigned positions and gifts that I've given them, and my Kingdom shall be more powerful than ever.

Everything you do and say according to my Word shall come to pass on the other side, which is this new life and direction of ministry and movement in your life. I've blessed you with this other side of ministry and movement in your life; don't allow anyone to tell you different.

Block out the naysayers and anyone that talk against you. Receive your wealthy place, your overflow, abundance, all sufficient and always abounding of money now, for being obedient and going to the other side. *This is the Word from God!*

June 17

Guard your heart. Speak evil of no man. I will reveal all things to you. Keep your mind and heart on me. I've given you the team to build my Kingdom. Focus on building them up in my Word. They're your help and they're with you to help build others up in my Word. There's

Things Seen in the Spirit

nothing you will have want or need of that they, your team, won't provide for you.

Watch out for the naysayers again. People bringing good news to you are secretly saying bad things about you; they throw rocks and hide their hands. Be wise, know who they are. Listen to Holy Spirit which shall help you and remove them from your presence. Continue building my Kingdom. I've given you wisdom, knowledge, and understanding. Souls shall continue to come through your wisdom. *This is the Word from God!*

He that hideth hatred with lying lips, and he that uttereth a slander, is a fool. (Proverbs 10:18)

A good man obtaineth favour of the Lord: but a man of wicked devices will he condemn. The way of a fool is right in his own eyes: but he that hearkeneth unto counsel is wise. The lip of truth shall be establish forever: but a lying tongue is but for a moment. Deceit is in the heart of them that imagine evil: but to the counselors of peace is joy. Lying lips are abomination to the Lord: but they that deal truly are his delight. (Proverbs 12:2, 15, 19-20, 22)

Now I beseech you, brethren mark them which cause divisions and offenses contrary to the doctrine which ye have learned; and avoid them. And the God of peace shall bruise Satan under your feet shortly. The grace of our Lord Jesus Christ be with you A-men. (Romans 16:17, 20).

Through wisdom is an house builded; and by understanding it is established. And by knowledge shall the chambers be filled with all precious and pleasant riches. (Proverbs 24:3-4)**June 20**

Jesus is the light that shines continually, Everlasting, Everywhere and Eternally. Follow this light and your paths will never be dark or dimmed. This light never goes out; it has an everlasting brightness and burning. This light, which is Jesus, flows and flashes from one point to another always reaching its Destination, and Delivering and Departing and Depositing what's needed at every dock.

If you allow Jesus to be your light, live and love in you, you'll have this light also. Your light will always shine that everyone sees your good works and glorify your Father which is in heaven. With the light of Jesus, no darkness can continue in your life and people can see their way through the storms of life, and receive the blessings of life. In the name of Jesus there's no more lack, theirs Spiritually minded people, demons trembling and fleeing, wealthy people, increase in the Kingdom, increase in your house, obedience, healing and wholeness, deliverance, no more confused minds, and most importantly love.

I gave you this light in my son. Always follow after Jesus and his example. My Holy Spirit shall lead, guide, teach and bring revelations through this light in my son. Trust and depend on me. I give you my angels, Holy Spirit and my son. I give you my best, which is my son, who paid it all for you.

So remember to give me your best in all that you do. I love you more and more, now you must remember to love more and more, even when things and people aren't loveable. You're blessed going in and blessed coming out. Your light isn't for you it's for others to See, and Seek, Serve and be Saved. I get all the glory. *This is the Word from God!*

June 23

I give you movement today and everyday of your lives. You must move away from the things and people that are not in my will. Move towards the things and people that are in my will. Every Word I say is true and every move I make is the right one. Watch your movement.

My Spirit shall lead, guide, teach, and give you remembrance of my Word. Therefore when you hear from him, do as he says, that is my Holy Spirit. My Spirit shall remind you that the move you made before wasn't a good one and not to make that move again.

Holy Spirit shall move you into great doors that I've already opened and allowed you to enter in. This is my holy place, your place of refuse and strength. Be confident in knowing I've placed you there. All mountains are removed; never to be replaced.

My Spirit is upon you; operate in the fullness of my ministry and blessings. Continue to make moves as my Spirit leads. Watch me move

Things Seen in the Spirit

on your behalf. Watch others move on your behalf. You shall move on behalf of others. We're all in this movement together.

Again I've given you this movement. Hear and listen to my Spirit, you shall always make the right moves. You're blessed going in and blessed coming out. Everywhere you move theirs Greatness, Gratitude, and Gaining and my Glory is revealed. *This is the Word from God!*

For our gospel came not unto you in word only, but also in power, and in the Holy Ghost, and in much assurance; as ye know what manner of men we were among you for your sake. And ye became followers of us, and of the Lord having received the Word in much affliction, with joy of the Holy Ghost: (1 Thessalonians 1:5-6)

This I say then, walk in the Spirit and ye shall not fulfill the lust of the flesh. If we live in the Spirit, let us also walk in the Spirit. (Galatians 5:16, 25)

And let us not be weary in well doing, for in due season we shall reap, if we faint not. (Galatians 6:9) *Continue in prayer, and watch in the same with thanksgiving;* (Colossians 4:2)

June 27

There's healing to all who believe and receive their healing. I've given you the power to lay hands on the sick and they're healed, including laying hands on yourself for your healing. Don't take back the sickness and disease I've healed you from. Never speak about past sickness and diseases coming back to you.

A dog never returns back to his vomit, you shouldn't either. You're my child and I'm your Father. I've given you proper training. I've raised you up, now you must train and help raise up my other children. You have all the necessary equipment and tools, never forget to use them. Never add your tools and equipment, they won't work properly. Every good and perfect gift come from me.

If I haven't said or done it, don't speak or do it. Don't except any bad report, believe my report, it's all good. I've given you a new song and praise in your mouth, many shall see it, and fear, and shall trust in me. Remember I have made this happen never forget; never go on your own.

You need me and I need you. I only work through willing vessels. Many shall be healed by your hands. Keep your hands and heart clean. Your gift isn't from man, they don't owe you, and you don't owe them. Money can't buy your hands. I've given you this love key; you must unlock every door where love is needed and wanted.

Don't force this key into unlock able doors, or doors that has bars. These doors are not to be opened by you. Your love key can only open bitterness, stubbornness, selfness, anger, malice and all evil attitudes if they've changed their locks to fit your key. *This is the Word from God!*

Whoso keepeth the fig tree shall eat the fruit thereof: so he waiteth on his master shall be honored. (Proverbs 27:18)

And he hath put a new song in my mouth, even praise unto our God; many shall see it, and fear, and shall trust in the Lord. And though I bestow all my goods to feed the poor, and though I give my body to be burned, and have not charity, it profiteth me nothing. (1 Corinthians 13:3)

He that hath clean hands, and a pure heart, who hath not lifted up his soul unto vanity, nor sworn deceitfully. (Psalm 24:4)

And when Paul had laid his hands upon them, and they spake with tongues, and prophesied. (Acts 19:6)

MONTH OF JULY

July 5

Check the people you have coming in your house and your space. What do they have on them? Are they anointed? Do they recognize the devil, and does the devil recognize them? Is the devil afraid of them, or is the devil comfortable around them?

When the devil comes in your house, he's afraid and he flees immediately. You recognize him and he recognizes you. You must continue to call him out and pray in the Holy Ghost that he never feels comfortable to return. Don't allow people to come in your house that don't recognize the devil, and the devil don't recognize them. Don't allow people to come in your house that's comfortable with the devil and he's comfortable with them. Make sure they have something on them, such as, the anointing, and Holy Spirit, helping them to discern and reveal all things to them.

As I have given you all these things, make sure you know I have given them these things also. Know who you have invited in your house and space. Don't allow anyone to deceive you, not the devil or his people. I gave you wisdom, I gave you my Word, and I gave you wealth.

This increase that I've given you isn't for you to invite anyone in your house or space that I've not told to be there. Your manifestation of monies and miracles are here now. You've asked and now you receive of me. Continue to keep my commandments and obey and serve me and love my people, you shall never be in want of my overflow and overtaking of my blessings. You will never lack again. *This is the Word from God!*

For many deceivers are entered into the world, who confess not that Jesus Christ, is come in the flesh. This is a deceiver and an antichrist. Look to yourselves, that we lose not those things which we have wrought, but that we receive a full reward. If there come any unto you, and bring not this doctrine, receive him not into your house, neither bid him God speed: For he that biddeth him God speed is partaker of his evil deeds. Let that therefore abide in you which ye have heard from the beginning. If that which ye have heard from the beginning shall remain in you ye also shall continue in the son, and in the Father. And this is the promise that he hath promised us, even eternal life. These things have I written unto you concerning them that seduce you. And whatever we ask, we receive of him, because we keep his commandments, and do those things that are pleasing in his sight. (1 John 3:22)

July 5

Scriptures of the Day: I have also spoken by the prophets, and I have multiplied visions, and used similitude's, by the ministry of the prophets. And by a prophet the Lord brought Israel out of Egypt, and by a prophet was he preserved. (Hosea 12: 10, 13)

I will stand upon my watch, and set me upon the tower, and will watch to see what he will say unto me, and what I shall answer when I am reproved. And the Lord answered me, and said, write the vision, and make it plain upon tables, that he may run that readeth it. For the vision is yet for an appointed time, but at the end it shall speak, and not lie: though it tarry, wait for it: because it will surely come, it will not tarry. (Habakkuk 2: 1-3)

July 8

I command you to build up my church this the body of baptized believers. They shall all be baptized in my Holy Spirit, with the evidence of speaking in tongues. You shall have apostles, prophets, evangelists, pastors, and teachers; to help build up and teach the saints, and to work in the ministry, and to edify the body of Christ.

I give you my best in your Pastor, as the leader of my church. Always follow after me, walk in love and love my people, which I trust in your hands. Speak boldly and preach my gospel. Pray always and in the Spirit, for all people.

Don't allow Satan to take anything from you and don't volunteer to give him anything. Again teach my people and work together. I'm sending many to your ministry and church every day. Go ye therefore.

Reach for the unreachable, according to what the world says. Go after the backslider, broken, and beat down. Build them up. Continue to build my people, and all who are oppressed.

If you teach my Word, and not yours, you will never go wrong. Teach sound doctrine, as my Spirit speaks and reveal to you. No souls shall be left behind. Souls are coming now, and shall continue to come in masses. *This is the Word from God!*

And I will give you pastors according to mine heart, which shall feed you with knowledge and understanding. (Jeremiah 3:15)

Praying always with all prayer and supplication in the Spirit, and watching thereunto with all perseverance and supplication for all saints. And for me, that utterance may be given unto me, that I may open my mouth boldly, to make known the mystery of the gospel. For which I am an ambassador in bonds; that therein I may speak boldly, as I ought to speak. (Ephesians 6:18-20)

Paul also and Barnabas continued in Antioch, teaching and preaching the Word of the Lord, with many others also. (Acts 15:35)

And so were the churches established in the faith, and increased in number daily. (Acts 16:5)

But I said, how shall I put thee among the children, and give thee a pleasant land, a goodly heritage of the hosts of nations? And I said, thou shalt call me, my Father, and shalt not turn away from me. Return, ye backsliding children, and I will heal your backslidings, behold, we come unto thee; for thou art the Lord our God. (Jeremiah 3:19, 22)

If thou wilt return, O Israel, saith the Lord, return unto me: and if thou wilt put away thine abominations out of my sight, then shalt thou not remove. (Jeremiah 4:1)

July 9

There's sheep in the midst of wolves. Pay attention to the wolves. Call them out. Don't let them play on and pervert your kindness. Let them know, theirs help if they want it, and they can be converted and changed from their conceiving ways. They will tell others that there is help for the hopeless and healing for the heart. The ones that do want help will tell others this isn't the place for Deception, but a place of Discerning, Deliverance, Developing and Dominion.

I gave you grace and peace and multiplied it through knowledge. You have my divine power and all things that pertain to life and Godliness. I've prepared and prompt you for the wolves and you know how to answer all mankind. You are my people and the sheep of my pasture.

Speak my Word, and when they don't hear you, shake the dust. Be watchful and pray and mindful of moving mouths, and mountains not moving. This is deception of the tongues of flattering women. They pretend to know me and they don't. Never be closed-minded, always be open-minded and hear my Spirit which will lead you into all things in life. *This is the Word from God!*

Beware of false prophets, which come to you in sheep's clothing, but inwardly they are ravening wolves. (Matthew 7:15)

Grace and peace be multiplied unto you through the knowledge of God, and of Jesus our Lord, According as his divine power given unto us all things that pertain unto life and Godliness, through the knowledge of him that hath called us to glory and virtue. (2 Peter 1:2, 3)

Know ye that the Lord he is God: it is he that hath made us, and not we ourselves; we are his people, and the sheep of his pasture. (Psalm 100:3)

Watch and pray that ye enter not into temptation: the Spirit indeed is willing, but the flesh is weak. (Matthew 26:41)

July 12

We should learn from the eyelid. When danger comes we automatically shut the door. Like mascara, when you accidentally stick the brush to close to the eyes they close immediately. When danger, problems and things not of God come to our mind, and heart, we should stop that thought. We shouldn't do what we want to do, but close the door to the things that's not going to advance or help us or the Kingdom. I created you to recognize and love Godly things, and hate the evil things. Walk in my will, and my Word, again you shall never fail. *This is the Word from God!*

July 18

I've given you the prayer of prophecy. This isn't a gift for everyone. You're open to receive and retain this gift. I know you'll be obedient to me and speak my Word and not yours. Always hear and listen to my Spirit.

Don't ever listen to the enemy. He comes as a wolf in sheep clothing. You must remove, replace, and refuse everything and everyone that's not speaking my language. Mark them, know who they are and put them away from you, even if it's your family.

Family can't understand where you are, and where you're going right now. Love them from afar. You have your best friend in your husband. I've made it this way because, friends can't understand and they will be envious and jealous. In time they shall see all my marvelous works and will know they had nothing to do with it. It's all me, your God, the one that loves you unconditionally. I know what I'm doing in you and I shall give you full understanding of what I'm doing in you.

Make sure in all your getting to get an understanding. You have my wisdom and knowledge and I shall continue to feed you more and more of me. This gift of prayer of prophecy shall be spoken to the nations.

People will hear from me through you and receive immediately, what they have need of; be it changed mind, healing, deliverance, increase and money. Yes even money! Believe my prophets so shall ye prosper. There's money in the mouth of the prophet.

You must be careful of who's in your house and heart, and who's in your space at all times. Don't make excuses why, because I've told you this. You owe no man anything but my Word. You've entered into my holiness of holies and you speak as my Spirit moves you to. You receive of me quickly and suddenly. You're blessed; you keep and receive my Words and my prophecies always. *This is the Word from God!*

Strengthen ye the weak hands, and confirm the feeble knees. Then the eyes of the blind shall be opened, and the ears of the deaf shall be unstopped. Then shall the lame man leap as a hart, and the tongue of the dumb sing; for in the wilderness shall waters break out, and streams in the desert. (Isaiah 35:3, 5-6)

This is the Word which the Lord hath spoken concerning him; (Isaiah 37:22a)

For the prophecy came not in old time by the will of man: but holy men of God spake as they were moved by the Holy Ghost. (2 peter 1:21)

Behold, I come quickly: blessed is he that kept the sayings of the prophecy of this book. (Revelation 22:7)

July 20

The Pouring – I. D. O. God says, he's pouring In, pouring Down, and pouring Out. He's pouring in his Word into our hearts and mind. He's pouring down manna from heaven, harvest of souls coming from everywhere and revelations like never before. He's pouring out overflowing of blessings, for the Kingdom and your house.

Your manifestation of money is here today, and something great is happening to you today. There's healing, deliverance, no more confusion in your mind, right decisions are made, and wrong decisions are corrected, increase of income, and order in your life, all happening to you today.

God's fulfilling every promise he's made and every prayer you prayed is answered today; even the prayers you prayed on this day. God is pouring out his Spirit on all those who will receive him now. *This is the Word from God!*

And the earth was without form, and void; and darkness was upon the face of the deep. And the Spirit of God moved upon the face of the waters. (Genesis 1:2)

For God is not the author of confusion, but of peace, as in all churches of the saints. Let all things be done decently and in order. (1 Corinthians 14:33, 40)

Confess your faults one to another, and pray one for another, that ye may be healed. The effectual fervent prayer of the righteous man availeth much. (James 5:16)

And it shall come to pass in the last days, saith God, I will pour out of my Spirit upon all flesh: and your sons and your daughters shall prophesy, and your young men shall see visions, and your old men shall dream dreams: (Acts 2:17)

July 20

Words from God! Five things about prayer and what role you play in fulfillment of prayers:

First: Prayer of Prophecy=Word from God;

Second: Prayer of Purpose=Commission from God;

Third: Prayer of Power= Ability from God;

Fourth: Prayer of Praise= Action from You;

Fifth: Prayer of Prosperity=Movement from You and Blessing from God.

JT blocks on AT7T U-Verse Yahoo Games; God have me a Word using this game as an example. The objective of the game is to click on the blocks which are the same color, two or more grouped together, and there's a special block you click on that will mix your colors to give you possibly more of the same colors, which gives you higher points.

You have five levels, with each level having a certain amount of points needed to reach each level. Last level is 18,750 points.

Gods says as believers we have different levels and goals to accomplish in our walk with him. We should seek after the higher level and don't stop until we get there. I reached level five and was 1,020 points away from winning the game. I told my husband, I won't stop until I get there and I wanted to see what the game looks like when I win. I will keep rising to the top. These were two different series he taught on at church. God says for us to set our affections on things above.

He also gave me a revelation in a sponge used for cleaning. When the sponge is dry it has no use for cleaning. When you spray the cleaning solution and water hits it, the sponge swells up after being wet. Now it'll clean properly.

Without God and his Word, prayer and praise you are no use. You must use your cleaning supplies, such as prayer and praise and get wet with the Word of God and swell up and activate the anointing in your life. Respond and receive all that God has promised you and to be a blessing and to be blessed. Build up his Kingdom first and you shall receive it all. *This is the Word from God!*

If ye then be risen with Christ, seek those things which are above, where Christ sitteth on the right hand of God. (Colossians 3:1)

Brethren, I count not myself to have apprehended: but this one thing I do, forgetting those things which are behind, and reaching forth unto those things which are before, I press toward the mark for the prize of the high calling of God in Christ Jesus. (Philippians 3:13-14)

But whosoever drinketh of this water shall thirst again: (John 4:14)

He brought me up also out of an horrible pit, out of the miry clay, and set my feet upon a rock, and established my goings. (Psalm 40:2)

But seek first the Kingdom of God, and His righteousness; and all these things shall be added unto you. (Matthew 6:33)

July 26

I see you walking around the gate but not entering in. You're confused and don't know which way is the entrance. You must gather your thoughts and take back control of your mind. Begin to hear and listen to me. I gave you a mind that's transformed and renewed and you gave it to the enemy. It's your job to get it back.

You have to do something about your condition, you chose this, and the devil didn't take it; you freely gave it to him. You have my Word in you and my power. Use what you got. Begin to obey and serve me now.

There's help when you ask for it. I won't force myself on you. You must receive what I have to offer you, which is repentance, and restoration, it's refreshing, receive now! Now you see clearly you shall enter into my gate; now you see the entrance, come in, I give you permission now.

Before you were weary and wondering. You finally took time to hear and listen to me, obey and gather your thoughts. You have taken charge over your mind and repented. Now you receive everything back which you so freely gave away. Don't be tricked, but train your thoughts to my thoughts. I only give you what you want. I won't force myself on you. Enjoy your freedom. *This is the Word from God!*

And Jesus answering said unto them, they that are whole need not a physician; but they that are sick. I came not to call the righteous, but sinners to repentance. (Luke 5:31-32)

I beseech you therefore, brethren, by the mercies of God, that ye present your bodies a living sacrifice, holy, acceptable unto God, which is your reasonable service. And be not conformed to this world: but be ye transformed by the renewing of your mind, that ye may prove what is that good, and acceptable, and perfect, will of God. (Romans 12:1-2)

For my thoughts are not your thoughts, neither are your ways my ways, saith the Lord. (Isaiah 55:8)

Enter into his gates with thanksgiving, and into his courts with praise; be thankful unto him, and bless his name. (Psalm 100:4)

Casting down imaginations, and every high thing that exalteth itself against the knowledge of God, and bringing into captivity every thought to the obedience of Christ; (2 Corinthians 10:5)

July 30

Word for Pastor A. D. Hatter: I've made you Pastor of 10,000 members, therefore, I give you land to house them. You shall build big. I give you favor with all people, saved and unsaved.

This new construction, the world and my people shall see. People will accept Jesus as their Lord and Saviour, when they see this great work. Some have to see my works to believe, let them see, I sent them to see and speak of me. I sent them there to bless you and the Kingdom. Except I build this house the laborers work is in vain.

Never be discouraged, disappointed or distracted. I shall complete my work and you shall complete yours. Teach my people, love my people, continue to obey and serve me, I shall bring it all to pass.

Don't worry about the money, mission or the mountains you come to. You must speak to the mountains and I shall remove them. Again do your part. Yes, I've given you this great reward, for the people to see me and for my Kingdom blessings and your blessings.

When the project gets heavy remember these Words, I'm speaking to you. I give you power to get wealth and the wealth of the wicked that was reserved for you it's your now. Receive the harvest now! Masses of souls are coming now!

Money is moving in your hands now! Manifestation of all material blessings is yours now! You've been faithful over the little things and monies. Now you're rulers over many. Everything you need and desire I give you now!

Always remember to be a good steward over your wealth and my people. This will cause you to keep and continue to receive more and more. This is your time of breakthrough favor; I give it all to you quickly, suddenly, and right now, as I've spoken in the past.

Lady Mary's book *T.S.I.T.S.* is seed money also to help build your new location for Kingdom Minded Church, and to build your new house. I shall cause all people to read her book and it shall be written in all different languages.

Everyone will hear my Words that I've spoken through her by my Spirit. I will pour out my Spirit on this world, to those that know me and to those that know me not, but receive me now. *This is the Word from God!*

Then I told of the hand of my God which was good upon me; as also the king's words that he had spoken unto me. And they said, let us rise up and build. So they strengthened their hands for this good work. (Nehemiah 2:18)

Give, and it shall be given unto you; good measure, pressed down, and shaken together, and running over, shall men give into your bosom. For with the same measure that ye mete withal it shall be measured to you again. (Luke 6:38)

But thou shalt remember the Lord thy God: for it is he that giveth thee power to get wealth, that he may establish his covenant which he swore unto thy fathers, as it is this day. (Deuteronomy 8:18)

For the Lord thy God bringeth thee into a good land, a land of brooks of water, of fountains and depths that spring out of valleys and hills; A land wherein thou shalt eat bread without scarceness, thou shalt not lack any thing in it; When thou hast eaten and art full, then thou shalt bless the Lord thy God for the good land which he hath given thee. Beware that thou forget not the Lord thy God, in not keeping his commandments, and his judgments and his statutes, which I command thee this day: (Deuteronomy 8: 7, 9-11)

Ask of me, and I shall give thee the heathen for thine inheritance and the uttermost parts of the earth for thy possession. (Psalm 2:8)

Thou shalt arise, and have mercy upon Zion: for the time to favour her, yea, the set time, is come. (Psalm 102:13)

July 31

Hear my Words, all ye people; use what I've blessed you with. You have my angels, Holy Spirit and my son. Forget not either one of them. Continue in my Word, obey and serve me, I shall bring it to pass. Everything you have need of and want is yours for the asking. I've spoken to you by my Spirit and revealed all things to you. Choose life and not death; choose the blessing and not the curse. I love you, and this is why I've given you my secrets, which are revealed by my Spirit and spoken by my prophets. *This is the Word from God!*

MONTH OF AUGUST

August 3

Pay close attention to those who have inherited the promises through faith and patience. Hear the voice of wisdom crying out to you. Get in the presence of those with money to learn and know how to get money. You have the money cometh anointing on your life.

Get in position to receive money now! As I gave to Abraham, so I give to you, as I said unto Moses, so I say unto you. Be wise with your money. Don't listen to foolish people, because they will continue to be broke.

Never be ashamed or make excuses about your wealth. People that are poor will talk about your wealth, but they will try to borrow. Only give to those I send to you. Don't waste your wealth on fools; they will say you haven't gotten this wealth from me.

Train and teach those that are as hungry as you are. Bless those that will be a blessing. Appreciate those that helped you to receive your wealth. Always be good stewards over your wealth and never keep back my portion. Continue to be a sower as I continue to give you seed. Wisdom is the principle thing; get wisdom and make sure you get understanding. *This is the Word from God!*

For God is not unrighteous to forget your work and labour of love, which ye have shewed toward his name, in that ye have ministered to the saints, and do minister. That ye be not slothful, but followers of them who through faith and patience inherit the promises. For when God made promise to Abraham, because he could swear by no greater, he sware by himself. Saying, surely blessing I will bless thee, and multiplying I will multiply thee. And so, after he had patiently endured, he obtained the promise. (Hebrews 6:10, 12-15)

Every place that the sole of your foot shall tread upon, that have I given unto you, as I said unto Moses. This book of the law shall not depart out of thy mouth; but thou shalt meditate therein day and night, that thou mayest observe to do according to all that is written therein: for then thou shalt make thy way prosperous, and then thou shalt have good success. (Joshua 1:3, 8)

The earth is the Lord's and the fullness thereof; the world, and they that dwell therein. He shall receive the blessing from the Lord, and righteousness from the God of his salvation. (Psalm 24:1, 5)

He that tilleth his land shall have plenty of bread: but he that followeth after vain persons shall have poverty enough. A faithful man shall abound with blessing; but he that maketh haste to be rich shall not be innocent. Wisdom is the principal thing; therefore get wisdom; and with all thy getting get understanding. (Proverbs 4:7)

August 5

These people, have I already revealed to you? Yes, they are the backbiters, backsliders, covenant breakers, idolaters, liars, fornicators, adulterers, wolves in sheep clothing, unsaved, drunkard, railers, thieves, hell raisers, and all manner of evil; don't keep company, and no, do not eat with such people. Don't be foolish; know that evil communications corrupt good manners. You shouldn't allow your good to be spoken evil of.

I called you to love my people and teach my people and also obey my Word in whole not in part. I've given you wisdom; learn of me and all that I do. Those that have a willing heart even in their falling down they rise back up. Those that are disobedient and won't hear me or keep my Words, shake the dust. I've showed you, who they are, know them and put them away from among you.

Forget about the foolish and live your life; go in the way of understanding as I told you to go. People will secretly hate you and lie on you and speak evil against you. They hate you for what I am to you and what you're to me, and they try to destroy you. I've created you to work for me and do good works, don't allow anyone to come in your space and surroundings, and hinder and hurt you and stop you from walking upright in them. *This is the Word from God!*

Be not deceived: evil communications corrupt good manners. (1 Corinthians 15:33)

But now I have written unto you not to keep company, if any man that is called a brother be a fornicator, or covetous, or an idolater, or a railer, or a drunkard, or an extortioner; with such an one no not to eat. But them that are without God judgeth. Therefore put away from among yourselves that wicked person. (1 Corinthians 5: 11, 13)

Now I beseech you, brethren mark them which cause divisions and offences contrary to the doctrine which ye have learned; and avoid them. For they that are such serve not our Lord Jesus Christ, but their own belly; and by good words and fair speeches deceive the hearts of the simple. (Romans 16:17-18)

Forsake the foolish, and live; and go in the way of understanding. (Proverbs 9:6)

He that hideth hatred with lying lips, and he that uttereth a slander, is a fool. (Proverbs 10:18)

A lying tongue hateth those that are afflicted by it; and a flattering mouth worketh ruin. (Proverbs 26:28)

For we are his workmanship, created in Christ Jesus unto good works, which God hath before ordained that we should walk in them. (Ephesians 2:10)

August 8

Darkness must come in order for light to come. Without darkness you couldn't count the days. Without dark situations you wouldn't appreciate the light or good situations. In your darkness there's always a little light.

Always know that darkness can't last forever. What you do with and in the light will determine what and how long the darkness will last. If you follow Jesus, which is the light of the world and your example, your darkness has to leave, which is Satan. Allow your Jesus, the light, to shine in you and you be the example, I can be glorified in darkness and light.

When you keep your light, which is Jesus shining; your dark or bad situations must become light or good situations. Make sure your darkness is temporary and you'll always receive the eternal light or life. *This is the Word from God!*

Let your light so shine before men that they may see your good works, and glorify your Father which is in heaven. (Matthew 5:16)

August 9

I give you Favor Givers. They bring CNN/MEDIA, into your life. They are: *Connected, Necessary,* and *Numbered.* They bring *Manifestation, Edification, Dominion, Increase,* and *Abundance.* I've *connected* them with you to help you reach the higher level of my blessings and promises to you.

They're *necessary* to give you wisdom and money to obtain all my work and wealth, which will help in winning souls and receiving your rewards. I've also *numbered* them and sent only a certain amount of them to you. These Favor-Givers speak my language and they confirm the things I've already spoken to you to reach your goals.

Make sure you receive wisdom, knowledge, and understanding. If one comes and you're not sure, ask me and I will give you clarity. In order to receive all that I've given you, pay attention and listen to them and do as they say, because they're receiving from me, as you receive from them. I've given them this assignment as you have been given yours, which is to build, teach, and love my people and you shall receive unlimited blessings. *This is the Word from God!*

August 10

Make sure you check the heart of the people that's in your space. If they love me and I'm in their hearts they will also love you and keep you in their hearts. Don't look at the outer appearance and trust in it. Check what's on the inside, and what's coming from the inside and going out, not the outside going in. If they don't have a heart for me they won't have a heart for you.

You have power in your speech. You call those things that are not as though they were. You speak to the mountain, not about the mountain. It shall obey you and be removed and casted away from you. Your problems obey your voice; tell them what you want them to do. You can let them stay, or call them gone. You are in control.

You choose to allow your problem to be small or great. You can allow it to be temporary or eternal. I've told you what to choose and that's life, not death with the power of your tongue. So take my choice or yours, because I come that you have life and life more abundantly. Continue in my Word keep them and live. *This is the Word from God!*

Blessed are the pure in heart for they shall see God. (Matthew 5:8)

He answered and said unto them, well hath E-sa'-ias prophesied of you hypocrites, as it is written, this people honoureth me with their lips, but their heart is far from me. There is nothing from without man, that entering into him can defile him: but the things which come out of him, those are they that defile the man. And he said, that which cometh out of the man, that defileth the man. (Mark 7:6, 15, 20)

A good man out of the good treasure of his heart bringeth forth that which is good; and an evil man out of the evil treasure of his heart bringeth forth that which is evil: for of the abundance of the heart his mouth speaketh. (Luke 6:45)

And he called the multitude, and said unto them, hear, and understand: (Matthew 15:10)

Death and life are in the power of the tongue: and they that love it shall eat the fruit thereof. (Proverbs 18:21)

I am come that they might have life, and that they might have it more abundantly. (John 10:10b)

August 11

I've taken you from behind the scenes and placed you in the front. Continue to humble yourselves before me. Never get puffed up in pride. Don't think of yourselves as highly as you ought to. What I've caused to go up, I can cause to come down. Receive your higher level in me.

I shall begin to speak to you in unknown places and about unknown things. I've chosen you because you are willing and want to hear me and do as I say. Your desire is to build up my kingdom; you have a heart for my people and you love me with all your heart, mind, body and soul. I pour out my Spirit on you now; you shall receive revelations like never before.

You shall begin to see people, places, names and situations before they come in your presence and before they are made known to the world. I shall speak to you on things to come in this world and my kingdom; you will be the voice of correction and clarity.

If the people hear and listen, they shall live and live in abundance. If they don't hear, they shall be in lack and finally destroyed. I've called you out from among the people, you're special and peculiar, my hand is on you; take me everywhere you go, even in places that's small and uncomfortable; I shall cause your places to be large and comfortable and everything your heart desires. Your children shall receive the same grace on them as you have received from Bishop I.V. Hilliard and Pastor Bridget Hilliard.

Again don't allow anyone in your space, I didn't put their; I've removed and will continue to remove anyone that you choose to be there, that I didn't send. Don't be confused or hurt; because you like them, they can't help you in the path I'm taking you. It's too much and they won't understand and be happy for you, they will be envious and jealous, which isn't my choice for you.

I've begun to send you help and likeminded people in your space and presence. I've centered you around wealthy people; they give you their wisdom and some of their wealth. I've even given you your material blessings from them too.

Don't give away or let anyone take what I've given and shall continue to bless you with. Receive my word and wealth today it's all yours. You've been faithful with little, I give you plenty now! You shall never be in lack or want again. *This is the Word from God!*

Humble yourselves therefore under the mighty hand of God, that he may exalt you in due time: (1 Peter 5:6)

For I say, through the grace given unto me, to every man that is among you, not to think of himself more highly than he ought to think; but to think soberly, according as God hath dealt to every man the measure of faith. (Romans 12:3)

Ye have not chosen me, but I have chosen you, and ordained you, that ye should go and bring forth fruit, and that your fruit should remain; that whatsoever ye shall ask of the father in my name, he may give it you. (John 15:16)

If ye be willing and obedient, ye shall eat the good of the land: (Isaiah 1:19)

We have also a more sure word of prophecy; whereunto ye do well that ye take heed, as unto a light that shineth in a dark place, until the day dawn, and the day star arise in your hearts: Knowing this first, that no prophecy of the scripture is of any private interpretation. For the prophecy came not in old time by the will of man: but holy men of God spake as they were moved by the Holy Ghost. (2 Peter 1:19-21)

But ye are a chosen generation, a royal priesthood, an holy nation, a peculiar people; that ye should shew forth the praises of him who hath called you out or darkness into his marvelous light: (1 Peter 2:9)

That ye be not slothful, but followers of them who through faith and patience inherit the promises. (Hebrews 6:12)

His Lord said unto him, well done, thou good and faithful servant: thou hast been faithful over a few things, I will make thee ruler over many things: enter thou into the joy of thy Lord. (Matthew 25:21)

August 13

Word from God! Wardrobe: As we look at our wardrobe, we check for things out of place, such as treads missing, strings hanging, stains and cleanliness. We should be the same when it comes to God and his kingdom.

We should check our prayer life, our praise and our intake of his word; and are we reading God's word, listening to his Word and doing what he says do? Are we loving his people, and building them up, and winning souls. We do all this checking of our wardrobe to make sure we like what we see and people like what they see.

We should make sure God likes what he sees and his people like what they see. We want to make sure we are pleasing in God's sight and glorify him with our daily lives. Words from God! WIFE: Wisdom, Increase, Favor, Enjoy; HUSBAND: Humble, Understanding, Security, Blessed, Authority, Never Deceiving.

August 14

Words from God! Toothpaste, Toothbrush, Mouthwash; Angels are like *toothpaste*, they assist and they are your helpers. Holy Spirit is like a *toothbrush*; he is your helper also. *Mouthwash* is like Jesus, he seals the deal, and all things happen in his name.

As your angels hearken unto your voice and ministers to you, and others, they bring what you ask of them. Without toothpaste your teeth can't get clean and germs won't be removed. Without angels working on your behalf, you won't receive what you're asking or commanding to come to pass in your life.

Without a toothbrush scrubbing away the germs and imperfections in your mouth you won't have total cleanliness. Without Holy Spirit revealing and showing you all the areas of germs and filthiness they won't get removed. Holy Spirit guides you so you scrub and brush away all uncleanliness.

Without mouthwash you won't get the full refreshing taste and smell you want and need. Without Jesus you won't receive all that's promised and provided for you. He's the one that causes you to receive it all from God in Jesus name.

The task is done. Make sure you use what you've been blessed with, which is angels, Holy Spirit, and Jesus, they all work together to help you get the job done and accomplished in your life. You are the little gods that allow them to all work together and use them as your helpers as they're necessary to edify and build up God's kingdom.

August 15

Scriptures of the Day: These things I have spoken unto you, that in me ye might have peace. In the world ye shall have tribulation; but be of good cheer; I have overcome the world. (John 16:33)

And said unto him, get thee out of thy country, and from thy kindred, and come into the land which I shall shew thee. This is that Moses, which said unto the children of Israel, a prophet shall the Lord your God raise up unto you do your brethren, like unto me; him shall ye hear. This is he, that was in the church in the wilderness with the angel which spake to him in the mount Si'-na, and with our Fathers; who received the lively oracles to give unto us: (Acts 7:3, 37-38)

But when they believed Philip preaching the things concerning the kingdom of God, and the name of Jesus Christ, they were baptized, both men and women. Then laid them their hands on them, and they received the Holy Ghost. (Acts 8:12, 17)

And he spake a parable unto them to this end, that men ought always to pray, and not to faint; Then Peter said, lo, we have left all, and followed thee. And he said unto them, verily I say unto you, there is no man that hath left house, or parents, or brethren, or wife, or children, for the kingdom of God's sake, Who shall not receive manifold more in this present time, and in the world to come life everlasting. (Luke 18:1, 28-30)

August 17

Words from God! Reason, Right, Receive, Rewards, Revealed, Revelations; You have a *reason* and a *right* to *receive* all the *rewards* and *revealed revelations*, not only in the Spiritual realm but the natural realm. I created you to be fruitful and multiply and replenish and subdue the earth.

You have a right to everything I've promised you, because you seek my kingdom first and my righteousness; therefore I've added all things unto you. In order to receive all your rewards you must do something.

Always remember to keep your faith in motion. When you receive one blessing don't stop. You've all sufficiency, abundance, and always abounding blessings. I've revealed revelations and all things to you. Don't stop hearing and listening to me and accomplishing your acquired tasks.

Continue in my Word, serve and obey me, I shall always bring It to pass. Whatever your It maybe. Remember without the seed their can't be a harvest. I speak the harvest has come, because of your seeds sown. *This is the Word from God!*

And God blessed them, and said unto them, be fruitful, and multiply, and replenish the earth, and subdue it: and have dominion over the fish of the sea, and over the fowl of the air, and over every living thing that moveth upon the earth. (Genesis 1:28)

But seek ye first the kingdom of God, and his righteousness; and all these things shall be added unto you. (Matthew 6:33)

And Jesus answering saith unto them, have faith in God. (Mark 11:22)

Know ye not that they which run in a race run all, but one receiveth the prize? So run, that ye may obtain. (1 Corinthians 9:24)

August 18

When you see this body of water, there is greenery, like grass, bushes, and trees. Everything that surrounds this body of water grows. This body is in the center and everything surrounds it. Jesus is the center of your life, and everything is surrounding him and connected to him grows. Without the body of water being the center and connecting the grass, bushes or trees they can't survive.

We should surround and connect ourselves to Jesus and allow him to increase in our lives and we will automatically experience growth. If this body of water dissolves or evaporate, everything connected or surrounded will die. Some die sooner than others.

Make sure your water and word of life don't get empty. With this water continuing and springing up, you will always grow and increase with the intake of God's Word. Live your life centered on the Word and allow Jesus to be the center of your life always. *This is the Word from God!*

For the wages of sin is death; but the gift of God is eternal life through Christ Jesus. (Romans 6:23)

But the water that I shall give him shall be in him a well of water springing up into everlasting life. (John 4:14b)

He that believeth on me, as the scripture hath said, out of his belly shall flow rivers of living water. (John 7:38)

August 26

Words from God! Posture, Planted, Position, Power; Stand, Solid, Straight, Strong; In order to serve me whole heartedly you must *posture* yourselves, be *planted*, and *positioned* to receive my *power*. You shall know how to *stand* in the evil days as well as the good days. Have and receive a *solid* word, so that your foundation stays *straight* and can't be shaken.

I've made you to be *strong* in me. Don't allow any false teachings or fake people to remove you from my place of provision, promotion, and prosperity. Winds, storms, floods, and fire will come; they only come to continue to strengthen you and help you on your journey to success in me.

Don't fear, have faith in me, I'm always with you, through the good and the bad; you shall prosper and always triumph. In good times you are able to help others as well as yourselves. Bad times, nothing shall be taken away from you and you're being prepared for the good times.

There are always blessings for you. I've loaded you with benefits. Remember to always *stand solid, straight* and *strong*. You have the *posture*, you're *planted, positioned* and have my *power* to get wealth, cast out devils and call all my promises to you and receive all your benefits and rewards now.

August 28

Word from God! Exit Row; Are you willing and cap able of sitting here and will you help others in the event of emergency? Are you able to help yourselves? This Exit Row is special being that it has extra space and costs more. I've placed you in this position. You have more than enough to work with.

There's a price you must pay to reside here. This is my special place and position, I've given you. Use what extras I've given you. Know it's not just for you but also to assist others. You must have their best interests at heart and help them to safety and secure the area of rescue. Check your order and security first then you can do the work I've prepared, placed and positioned you for.

Always have my people on your mind; cover and have compassion for them, so that you both win in tough and emergency times. Don't panic, stay calm, continue to hear and listen to me? You will always do and receive my instructions in the order that I give. In this Exit Row there are things you need to prepare, for the emergency exit.

You must also do things descent and in order. Have a safe exit. Take me with you always on this journey and others also. I will always have your back. Don't look back you have done your job successfully. I'm well pleased. Get ready for the next stop.

August 29

Words from God! Passing Process: This too shall pass. Everything that you are going through, it's for my sake. You are *passing* through this *process* of, provisions, promotions and promises. I've allowed this order of Passing Process.

This will not hurt you, but help you. You will not be stuck in the valley but pass through the valley of this process, of provisions, promotions, and promises. Don't be weary in well doing, you shall reap and faint not.

You have been restored of everything that was stolen from you. You have my word, count on my word, I never make a promise I can't and won't keep. Agree with me I shall bring it to pass, as I have spoken before. Trust me in all I do and say to you.

You shall see me in the little things that I've already provided for you. I've spoken to you by my Spirit and your spiritual father and mother, which are Bishop I.V. Hilliard and Pastor Bridget Hilliard.

Always stay tuned to my station; I'm always on the airwaves. Stay tuned for future instructions; follow my instructions just as I speak them. Always have ears to hear what I say and do as I say, not as you want to do. Your blessings shall continue to flow, even in your testing, trials and testimony times. *This is the Word from God!*

He restoreth my soul: he leadeth me in the paths of righteousness for his name sake. Yea, though I walk through the valley of the shadow of death, I will fear no evil: for thou art with me; thy rod and thy staff they comfort me. (Psalm 23:3-4)

Hear instruction, and be wise, and refuse it not. For whoso findeth me findeth life, and shall obtain favour of the Lord (Proverbs 8:33, 35)

August 30

Words from God! Fire and Smoke; Fire either purifies or burns. Smoke is evidence there is or was a fire. Smoke is dark, black and gray. Dark and black shows the fire is bad or at its worst and will bring ashes. Gray shows the fire is light or going away, or the fire isn't that bad anymore and you can salvage some things left afterwards.

The fire that purifies shows that some things can't be burned. You shall come out as pure gold. Gold can't be burned. Holy Spirit is a fire that never burns out. He allows and helps you to keep going when your mind and body wants to stop. He helps you to endure to the end. He brings the rain when the fire with smoke is present.

Receive the fire that I bring and baptize you with; my Holy Spirit which will not drown you when you go through deep waters and when you go through the fire that brings smoke. You won't be burned and the smoke can't consume or overtake you; I give you extra help with my Son Jesus and the fire of the Holy Spirit. I do this because I love you and have great things waiting for you, which you must see and believe I've prepared these things before they are made manifest in your life.

Holy Spirit gives you my wisdom, knowledge and understanding of the great things to come. I chose you for such a time as this. I gave you your helper, which is Holy Spirit; allow him to help you so you can help others to receive the finer things in life; which eyes have not seen nor ears heard, which God has prepared for them that love him. *This is the Word from God!*

I indeed baptize you with water unto repentance: but he that cometh after me is mightier than I, whose shoes I am not worthy to bear: he shall baptize you with the Holy Ghost, and with fire: (Matthew 3:11)

And they were all filled with the Holy Ghost, and began to speak with other tongues, as the Spirit gave them utterance. (Acts 2:4)

When thou passest through the waters, I will be with thee; and through the rivers, they shall not overflow thee: when thou walkest through the fire, thou shalt not be burned; neither shall the flame kindle upon thee. (Isaiah 43:2)

But the manifestation of the Spirit is given to every man to profit withal. (1 Corinthians 12:7)

But as it is written, eye hath not seen, nor ear heard, neither have entered into the heart of man, the things which God hath prepared for them that love him. (1 Corinthians 2:9)

MONTH OF SEPTEMBER

September 2

You are my candle and my light. You shall not be blown out or turned off. You shall shine in places where there's has never been light. You shall continue to burn even though the winds blow. I placed you on this mantle; no one can remove you but you.

You see from the top down. Your light is brighter from above. If you choose to replace and reposition yourself your fire will burn out immediately. You won't survive down low; you've been positioned up high. Keep your position, your place, and your power.

You're my beautiful wax that I've shaped and formed and allowed to burn. I had you on my mind even before you were born. Know your place and keep your place on high. You were made for this mantle, you're on display to others that they see your works through the light shining in your beautifulness, and I shall always be glorified.

Your light shall never be hidden. Your light shines even in darkness. Darkness will come, but your light shall out shine the darkness. Never look at darkness as your enemy. See darkness as your process of promises and promotions. Remember you are still light; darkness doesn't change your status and stance, I've given you power to keep your light on so never turn it off. *This is the Word from God!*

Arise, shine; for thy light is come and the glory of the Lord is risen upon thee. For, behold, the darkness shall cover the earth, and gross dark-

ness the people: but the Lord shall arise upon thee, and his glory shall be seen upon thee. (Isaiah 60:1-2)

And he said unto them, is a candle brought to be put under a bushel, or under a bed? And not to be set on a candlestick? For there is nothing hid, which shall not be manifested; neither was anything kept secret, but that it should come abroad. (Mark 4:21-22)

Let your light so shine before men that they may see your good works, and glorify your father which is in heaven. (Matthew 5:16)

September 8

On these two great commandments hang all the law and the prophets. Love me with all your heart, soul and mind; love your neighbor as thyself. Never exalt yourself but humble yourself and you shall be exalted.

When you have a heart, soul and mind that love me, you love my people; you keep my Word and do everything as unto me. I created, called and chose you; I didn't make a mistake in the matter. You are mine, I send you out to do my work. Rely on me I shall bring it all to pass.

Don't forget, remember to always work while the work can be done, when the end comes no one and no work can be done. Souls are saved by your working, kingdoms are built by your working, families are restored and rebuilt by your working, husbands and wives are in agreement by your working, and the body of baptized believers are edified and built up by your working.

You receive your rewards, blessings, and my promises by your working. Keep these two commandments always; they're the path, pattern, principles, and process to your promised promotions and provisions. *This is the Word from God!*

Jesus said unto him, thou shalt love the Lord thy God with all thy heart, and with all thy soul, and with all thy mind. This is the first and great commandment. And the second is like unto it, thou shalt love thy neighbor as thyself. On these two commandments hang all the law and the prophets. (Matthew 22:37-40)

And whosoever shall exalt himself shall be abased; and he that shall humble himself shall be exalted. (Matthew 23:12)

Ye have not chosen me, but I have chosen you, and ordained you, that ye should go and bring forth fruit, and that your fruit should remain; that whatsoever ye shall ask of the father in my name, he may give it you. (John 15:16)

And whatsoever ye do in word or deed, do all in the name of the Lord Jesus, giving thanks to God and the father by him. (Colossians 3:17)

September 9

Scriptures of the Day: As obedient children, not fashioning yourselves according to the former lusts in your ignorant: But as he which hath called you is holy, so be ye holy in all manner of conversation; Because it is written, be ye holy; for I am holy.

But with the precious blood of Christ, as of a lamb without blemish and without spot; being born again, not of corruptible seed, but which liveth and abideth forever. (1 Peter 1:14-16, 19, 23)

For I will pour water upon him that is thirsty, and floods upon the dry ground: I will pour my spirit upon thy seed, and my blessing upon thine offspring: Thus saith the Lord the king of Israel, and his redeemer the Lord of hosts; I am the first, and I am the last, and beside me there is no God; (Isaiah 44:3, 6)

And I will give thee the treasures of darkness, and hidden riches of secret places, that thou mayest know that I, the lord, which call thee by thy name, am the God of Israel. That they may know from the rising of the sun, and from the west, that there is none beside me. I am the Lord, and there is none else. I formed the light, and create darkness: I make peace, and create evil: I the Lord do all these things. (Isaiah 45: 3, 6-7)

September 14

There are certain parts of your body I use to get my Word to you and my people. I use your mouth, tongue and lips; not your teeth, even though they are part of your mouth. When you put your teeth together your lips and tongue still moves and you can still speak.

Even though you might be deaf and can't hear with your ears, or speak with your mouth, you hear me through your mind, and from the hands of others I give you signs language to hear me. As you have hands signs, I give you spoken words through my teachers, pastors, preachers, and prophets.

You see it doesn't matter how I use you, but that you allow me to use you. I chose you as one of my faithful remnant. Don't be concern about what others think of you, say about you, or do to you. If I allow certain parts of your body to function even without the other parts that holds them together, what do you think I can do with the wicked and evil doers?

Remember not to use your mouth or tongue to speak lies, be deceitful or any other sin. I shall undo all that afflict you. I shall bring you into this time now, and give you a name and praise among all people of the earth, when I turn back your enemies before your eyes. *This is the Word from God!*

A wholesome tongue is a tree of life: but perverseness therein is a breach in the Spirit. The lips of the wise disperse knowledge: but the heart of the foolish doeth not so. (Proverbs 15:4, 7)

September 18
Words from God! PDF; Peace, Deliverance, Finance

September 21
Let nothing *interrupt, interfere* and *invade* what I called you to do for me. I gave you this work in my kingdom and it shall be done. I'm bigger better and brighter than anything or anyone that's in your life. Continue to meditate day and night, hear and listen to me.

When I speak it's the *sound* and *supernatural supply* from me. You have received the sound and supernatural supply; which is abundance, always abounding and all sufficiency of favor and grace. Walk in my perfect will for your life; it's been a *struggle*, but you *survived*, you're *strong* in me.

You didn't forget to *stand* in the evil times. Enjoy, it's my pleasure to give you this wealth; you have been faithful in your waiting and working for me and my people. The best is yet to come. *This is the Word from God!*

September 28

Words from God! Faith, Freedom, Focus, Friend; I've caused you to hear me like never before. Continue to hear my Word and no other word. I am the God that knows you and you know me.

Stay in *faith* and receive my *freedom. Focus* on the ministry I've called you too. Give no one a reason to say what I'm not or have not done in your life or the ministry. My Word is fulfilled in you and your works. Continue to have *faith, freedom, focus*, because you have my gift of righteousness and it is I that call you *friend. This is the Word from God!*

So then faith cometh by hearing, and hearing by the word of God. (Romans 10:17)

And ye shall know the truth and the truth shall make your free. (John 8:32)

Giving no offence in anything that the ministry be not blamed: (2 Corinthians 6:3)

And the scripture was fulfilled which saith, Abraham believed God, and it was imputed unto him for righteousness; and he was called the friend of God. (James 2:23)

MONTH OF OCTOBER

October 4

Words from God! Order, Obedience, Overflow; Let all things be done decently and in order. (1 Corinthians 14:40)

If ye be willing and obedient, ye shall eat the good of the land: (Isaiah 1:19)

Thou anointed my head with oil; my cup runneth over. (Psalm 23:5b)

October 8

Just like you go to work, you fight through the crowds, the traffic and you expect a pay check for your work. You are always making an effort to get there on time, and do what's required of you on the job. In all that you do for the job, I deserve that and more.

When you seek my kingdom first and my righteousness, I add everything else unto you. *Fighting* through the crowds, I give you *favour*. Getting through the *traffic*, I allow you to *triumph*. *Expecting* a paycheck, I give you *exceeding*, abundantly, above all you can ask or think.

Your job is to hear me, do what I say, speak my Word, keep my Word, and bring others into my kingdom, and teach them; and they teach others and you are always abounding in good works. *This is the Word from God!*

The wealth of the wicked is yours now! Seedtime is your *favour*, *fruit*, and *financial* harvest now! Increase and income is yours now!

Your barns are filled with plenty; I've made you fat! I give you keys to the kingdom now! In my house you shall receive many mansions now!

Wealth and riches are in your house now! You shall never be in lack another day in your life! Receive your overflow and outpouring of my spirit now! All that I send to you pray the prayer of *release, renew, revenue, render, righteousness, revelation, refreshing,* and *receiving* on them. I give the command, you obey and serve me, I will cause people to obey and serve you. They shall give you the honour that's due.

You have labored with me and continue to labor, your work shall never be in vain. Continue your work while its day, when night comes no one can work. This is your time, as I have already spoken to you; your set time of favour is here, because you favour my righteous cause.

Receive your manifestation of souls, Things Seen In The Spirit, more money in your hands than you ever had before, and revelations and rewards like never before. The blessings are yours now! All my promises, receive them now! You shall never be in lack or want ever again. Keep my Word in your heart, do as I say, hear me and all that I've given you shall be everlasting and eternally. *This is the Word from God!*

Thou shalt arise, and have mercy upon Zion: For the time to favour her, yea, the set time, is come. (Psalm 102:13)

Let them shout for joy, and be glad, that favour my righteous cause: Yea, let them say continually, let the Lord be magnified, which hath pleasure in the prosperity of his servant. (Psalm 35: 27)

October 15

Scriptures of Day; To appoint unto them that mourn in Zion, to give unto them beauty for ashes, the oil of joy for mourning, the garment of praise for the spirit of heaviness; That they might be called trees of righteousness, the planting of the Lord, that he might be glorified. And their seed shall be known among the gentiles, and their offspring among the people: all that see them shall acknowledge them, that they are the seed which the Lord hath blessed. (Isaiah 61:3, 9)

For God is not unrighteous to forget your work and labor of love, which ye have shewed toward his name, in that ye have ministered to the saints, and do minister. That ye be not slothful, but followers of them who through faith and patience inherit the promises. Saying, surely blessing I will bless thee, and multiplying I will multiply thee. And so, after he had patiently endured, he obtained the promise. (Hebrews 6:10, 12, 14-15)

Wherefore he is able also to save them to the uttermost that come unto God by him, seeing he ever liveth to make intercession for them. (Hebrews 7:25)

October 18

Spiritual Menu
Three Types of Liquids

First: Oil of God
Second: Blood of Jesus
Third: Water Baptism and Holy Spirit

Twelve Items of Foundation

One Solid	Two Sides
1. Faith Romans 10:17; Joshua 1:8	Hearing & Actions
2. Grace Romans 5:21; 2 Corinthians 5:21	Favor & Righteousness
3. Peace Isaiah 26:3; Philippians 4:7	Mind & Understanding
4. Mercy 16:6; Psalm 23:6	Truth & Goodness *Proverbs*
5. Power Ephesians 6:10; Luke 6:19	Strength & Authority
6. Prosperity 3 John 1:2; Psalm 35:27	Souls & Pleasure
7. Promise 2 Corinthians 1:20; Matthew 18:19	Yes & Agreement
8. Prayer Matthew 21:22-24	Asking & Believing
9. Praise Psalm 35:28; Psalm 150:6	Speaking & Outward Expression
10. Prophecy Revelation 22:7	Revealed & Knowledge *Amos 3:7;*
11. Pastor 1 Corinthians 13:2; Hebrews 13:17	Loving & Teaching
12. Kingdom 2 Peter 1:11	Ruling & Reigning

I've given you everything you need in my *Spiritual Menu*. You have liquids first; starting with my oil, the blood of Jesus, and you're baptized in water along with Holy Spirit. You have my solids and sides.

These are twelve items of foundation. If you start with faith first and receive all in the middle, which I've released to you; you will end up with my kingdom being built the way I intended and want it to be built.

My kingdom shall rule and reign on earth and in heaven. You are a part of making this happen; when you follow through, display, do, and order from my *Spiritual Menu*. When you receive your order, there's no cost from me. You only pay if you don't order what's on my menu. *This is the Word from God!*

October 18

I give you Insight, Invision, Intercession, Intellect, Inventions, Interception, Invasion, Income and Increase. All these work together for your good, because you love me and are the called according to my purpose. I allow you to see and I give you an inside look at the things and people that are coming and what's going to happen when they come.

You are to pray for the things and people I've shown you ahead of time. I've made you smart and I've given you inventions. I give you power to intercept and invade anything and anyone that tries to stop what I've placed, positioned, promised, and provided for you and my people. Because of your obedience and keeping my word and doing as I said, you have entered into my place of wealth and wisdom.

Never be puffed up in pride. Help those I send your way; and they shall be blessed in Word and in deed. Many shall come for you to teach and show them how to receive of me. You have blessings of income and increase. Enjoy the ride and never stop. This is an ongoing process; continue to do what you did to get here. *This is the Word from God!*

October 21

When you are in the shoe store, either you are going to get in line and purchase the shoes and enjoy wearing them; or you will get out of line and put them back on the shelf and someone else will but them. In the kingdom you must choose to take God's word, apply it in your life and live prosperous; or put it down and someone else will live in the the wealth and wisdom of God. *This is the Word from God!*

October 24

Continue to walk in love and joy. I love you as I love my son, Jesus. I'm glorified when you bare much fruit and you are my disciples. If you keep my commandments you shall abide in love.

I've spoken to you that my joy might remain in you and that your joy might be full. Love one another, as I have loved you. I gave you greater love when I allowed my son to give his life for you, his friends. You are my friends if you keep my commandments.

I give you my Spirit to lead and guide you into all truths. He shall speak and whatever you hear, that's what you shall speak; and he'll shew you things to come. Make sure you ask of me, but in my son, Jesus name, and I will give it to you; you shall receive and your joy will be full. *This is the Word from God!*

Herein is my father glorified, that ye bear much fruit; so shall ye be my disciples. As the father hath loved me, so have I loved you: Continue ye in my love. If ye keep my commandments, ye shall abide in my love; Even as I have kept my father's commandments, and abide in his love.

These things have I spoken unto you, that my joy might remain in you, and that your joy might be full. This is my commandment, that ye love one another, as I have loved you. *This is the Word from God!*

Greater love hath no man than this that a man lay down his life for his friends. Ye are my friends, if ye do whatsoever I command you. (John 15:8-14)

And in that day ye shall ask me nothing. Verily, verily, I say unto you, whatsoever ye shall ask the father in my name, he will give it you.

Hitherto have ye asked nothing in my name: ask, and ye shall receive, that your joy may be full. (John 16: 23-24)

October 25

Your life is like a Circle and Compass. In both of these there is a beginning and an ending. They have a direction which cause for movement. I've given you these examples because you should know this; how you begin your direction and movement will determine how and what your end will be. Just like your faith in me and following me will determine your finish.

Check who's in your circle and set the compass to the direction you want to go. Make sure it's according to my wisdom and word that I've given you. Knowing who's in your circle is key. You are the commander and coach of this journey. Choose who you will serve and surrender to and who you will allow to help or hinder you.

Will you choose the team I've chosen? Or will you choose your own? Choose my team, you finish. Choose your team you're stuck in the middle; and you can't go back and you can't go forward.

When I choose your *circle* and set your *compass* it's for completion. When you choose and let others set your direction you never finish. Know that you have four things that complete your circle and directions you must go, according to your compass.

First is Prayer, Second is Praise, Third is Power and Fourth you receive your Promises and reach your destination. Without prayer, praise and power you won't see promises or get to your destination. Make sure you hear from me on the people you allow in your circle, the setting of the compass and direction of where you're going and where you will end up. If you know the circle I've called you to and the compass I've set for you; you will never fall.

Follow my plan, this is your position and place I've set you in. Don't allow anyone or anything to lead you in the wrong direction; and you will make it to your destination. In the end you have my outpouring of prayer, praise, power, peace, promises, promotions and prosperity. *This is the Word from God!*

And whatsoever ye do, do it heartily, as to the Lord, and not unto men; (Colossians 3:23)

And unto him that is able to do exceeding abundantly above all that we ask or think, according to the power that worked in us. (Ephesians 3:20)

Wherefore the rather, brethren, give diligence to make sure your calling and election sure: for if ye do these things, ye shall never fall. (2 peter 1:10)

For all the promises of God in him are yea, and in him A-men, unto glory of God by us. (2 Corinthians 1:20)

Now thanks be unto God, which always causeth us to triumph in Christ, and maketh manifest the Savour of his knowledge by us in every place. (2 Corinthians 2:14)

October 26

It's already done. It's in your house, hands, and heart. I've given you creative ideas and witty inventions. I've even given you my word to speak to the nations. Use what you got.

Believe my word and receive your wealth. Wealth and riches are in your house now! Trust me it was I that spoke before and it's I that's speaking now. It's on you, it's yours. You asked me, it's according to my Word, and I want you to receive all that you've asked me for. I've even given you some extras.

You have reaped where you haven't sown. I'm so pleased to give you exceedingly abundantly above all that you can ask or think blessings. I give you everything that eyes hath not seen, nor ears heard, neither have entered into your heart, the things that I've prepared and promised you because of your love for me.

It has already been revealed by my spirit. I spoke it through your mentor and spiritual father, Bishop IV Hilliard. I poured it out on you at the conference.

Again I say it's you. You've been conditioned for the road and conditioned for the ride, enjoy. You gave your sacrifice seed; it has opened the door for the overflow and outpouring of all your promises, provisions, and promotions. *This is the Word from God!*

But as it is written, eye hath not seen, nor ear heard, neither have entered into the heart of man, the things which god hath prepared for them that love him. But God hath revealed them unto us by his Spirit: for the Spirit searcheth all things, yea, the deep things of God. (1 Corinthians 2:9-10)

MONTH OF NOVEMBER

November 1

Let there be and it became. As I have spoken in the beginning and this world was created; so shall you speak and receive all that I have prepared and promised you. You have dominion over all these things that I've spoken and created; you haven't lost you status. Trust me and do as I've said and continue to say; you shall continue to receive all these things you've spoken according to my word.

This is my Word that will never go empty, it'll always do as I please and cause prosperity in where ever I send it. My Word is always true; never receive any word that I've not spoken. The words of false teachers will keep you bound; but you know my Word and you have freedom.

I'm removing the naysayers and negative people, places, and things out of my kingdom and your life! Beware of them, know who they are remove them out as I reveal them to you; don't replace them, because they don't want to be restored in me. Remember I made you and I didn't make them to do the things they're doing. They have their own maker they have chosen to follow.

Be watchful and pray; but as I move, you move just like that. Just do it. Don't question me, when I say something it's true. Believe my prophets, when they speak it's from me, because what they speak comes to pass. *This is the Word from God!*

November 2

Words from God! Captured, Covered, Closed; Don't be afraid of what the enemy tries to do to you. I've captured your enemies; you're covered by the blood of Jesus; and everything the devil has tried and will try again it's closed. I shut him down. Know and remember, I'm your God. I'm your strength, sustainer, source, supplier, and security.

You have my PDF! This is the format that the world uses for documents. This is the format I give you for the world to see you're blessed. I give you Peace Deliverance and Finance in that order. *Peace* that surpasses all understanding, *deliverance* out of hands of your enemies and *finances* in abundance; as long as you keep my Words and do as I have commanded. *This is the Word from God!*

And he said, hearken ye, all Judah, and ye inhabitants of Jerusalem, and thou king Jehoshaphat, thus saith the Lord unto you, be not afraid nor dismayed by reason of this great multitude; for the battle is not yours but God's. Ye shall not need to fight in this battle: set yourselves, stand ye still, and see the salvation of the Lord with you, o Judah and Jerusalem: fear not, nor be dismayed; tomorrow go out against them: for the Lord will be with you. (2 Chronicles 20:15; 17)

If ye walk in my statutes, and keep my commandments, and do them; Then I will give you rain in due season and the land shall yield her increase, and the trees of the field shall yield their fruit. And I will give peace in the land, and ye shall lie down, and none shall make you afraid: and I will rid evil beasts out of the land, neither shall the sword go through your land. And ye shall chase your enemies, and they shall fall before you by the sword. And five of you shall chase an hundred, and an hundred of you shall put ten thousand to flight: and your enemies shall fall before you by the sword. For I will have respect unto you, and make you fruitful, and multiply you, and establish my covenant with you. And I will walk among you, and will be your God, and ye shall be my people. (Leviticus 26:3-4, 6-9, 12)

November 7

Reflecting, Remembering, and Recalling all our past and present failures, especially in the area of finances. I allowed you to see where you will never result back to again; and for you to see where you are and that you are not staying in this condition.

I've prepared, promised and provided you with an outpouring of prosperity like never before. You shall receive, retain, and reap all your revenue and rewards right now, this day, your manifestations; especially more monies than you ever had in your hands before.

Never return to your past of present failures, because you have a right now faith as well as finances and future fortunes. Always remember it's I that caused you to get this wealth. Put me first at all times and and you shall never go empty; you shall always be abounding, and having more than enough. *This is the Word from God!*

November 8

Scriptures of the Day: Then they cry unto the Lord in their troubles and he bringeth them out of their distresses. He maketh the storm calm, so that the waves thereof are still. Then are they glad because they be quiet; so he bringeth them unto their desired haven. Oh that men would praise the Lord for his goodness, and for his wonderful works to the children of men! Let them exalt him also in the congregation of the people, and praise him in the assembly of the elders. He turneth the wilderness into a standing water, and dry ground into water springs. And there he maketh the hungry to dwell, that they may prepare a city for habitation; And sow the fields, and plant vineyards, which may yield fruits of increase. He blesseth them also, so that they are multiplied greatly; and suffereth not their cattle to decrease. Whosoever is wise, and will observe these things, even they shall understand the lovingkindness of the Lord. (Psalms 107:28-32, 35-38, 43)

November 12

Be strong in me and in my power. I've given you wisdom, knowledge and understanding. With wisdom you have built your house and by understanding it is established: by knowledge your house is filled with all precious and pleasant riches.

You're wise and strong; and your knowledge increaseth strength. Remember not to faint in the day of adversity, because your strength will be made small. Your wisdom is too high for a fool; and the thoughts of foolishness is sin.

Don't say to evil you will do so to him, as he hath done to you: I will render to the man according to his work. Believers don't fight against each other: because your enemies are together laughing at you.

Continue to give me praise in and through it all. You hath the victory, the power and a willing heart: never lose heart; I shall always be with you even in your trying times. Expect the great even if it don't look great. *This is the Word from God!*

November 14

G.R.E.A.T.! Give, to Receive, Exceedingly, Abundantly, above all you can ask or Think; I've made you to be a giver. In order to give, you must have received something. When you are willing and obedient you eat the good of the land; this land flows with milk and honey.

This land has what's needed and it prospers. You must make sure you dress it, keep it; and it multiplies, it's fruitful and replenished. Allow others to live in this land as I have called them there. Don't allow any ravens or vulchers to eat in this land; or else the land be done away with. This land is G.R.E.A.T.!

I allowed you to come here. I trust you to do what's right and rule here. Don't give away what I granted so graciously to you. I've given you control, you're in charge of where I called and chosen you to be.

Remember I'm the head of the land, I made it; you have dominion over it. Always hear and listen and do as I instruct; you will never fail. Again, I say I've blessed you to be a blessing. In order to be a giver; you must have received something to give.

We both must do our part in the giving process. I allow men to give to you, and you give to those I send to you. Plant my seed, where it meets the need continually; and you shall never be in lack. My soil, as long as it's planted and watered shall always yield increase from me. *This is the Word from God!*

Now unto him that is able to do exceeding abundantly above all that we ask or think, according to the power that worketh in us, (Ephesians 3:20)

If ye be willing and obedient ye shall eat the good of the land: (Isaiah 1:19)

And God said, let us make man in our image, after our likeness: and let them have dominion over the fish of the sea, and over the fowl of the air, and over the cattle, and over all the earth, and over every creeping thing that creepeth upon the earth. And God blessed them, and God said unto them, be fruitful, and multiply, and replenish the earth, and subdue it: and have dominion over the fish of the sea, and over the fowl of the air, and over every living thing that moveth upon the earth. (Genesis 1: 26, 28)

Therefore thou shalt keep the commandments of the Lord thy God, to walk in his ways, and to fear him. A land wherein thou shalt eat bread without scarceness, thou shalt not lack any thing in it; When thou hast eaten and art full, then thou shalt bless the Lord thy God for the good land which he hath given thee. But thou shalt remember the Lord thy God: for it is he that giveth thee power to get wealth. (Deuteronomy 8:6, 9-10, 18)

I have planted, Apollo's watereth; but God gave the increase. (1 Corinthians 3:6)

November 17

Words from God! What shall I render unto the Lord for all his benefits towards me? (Psalm 116:12)

Thanks, Praise, and Prayer: It is a good thing to give thanks unto the Lord, and to sing praises unto thy name, O most high: (Psalm 92:1)

I will declare thy name unto my brethren: in the midst of the congregation will I praise thee. (Psalm 22:22)

O give thanks unto the Lord; for he is good: because his mercy endureth for ever. (Psalm 118:1)

I will offer to thee the sacrifice of thanksgiving, and will call upon the name of the Lord. I will pay my vows unto the Lord in the presence of all his people. (Psalm 116:17-18)

Praise ye the Lord. Praise God in his sanctuary: Praise him in the firmament of his power. Praise him for his mighty acts; praise him according to his excellent greatness. (Psalm 150:1-2, 6)

Let everything that hath breath praise the Lord. Praise ye the Lord. (Psalm 122:6)

Pray for the peace of Jerusalem; they shall prosper that love thee. Hearken unto the voice of my cry, my king, and my God: for unto thee will I pray. My voice shalt thou hear in the morning, O Lord; in the morning will I direct my prayer to thee and will look up. (Psalm 5:2-3)

Pray without ceasing. In everything give thanks: for this is the will of God in Christ Jesus concerning you. (1 Thessalonians 5:17-18)

November 26

I'm a God that's everywhere at the same time and I can bless everyone at the same time. Just like I make sun to shine in the south, snow to fall in the north, rain in the east, and sleet in the west; it's my choice to do as I please.

You need the clouds to bring rain, and the rays to bring the sun. You need my Word mixed with faith; and I shall bring it to pass. Whatever you have need of it's in my Word: my principles brings the plan and process to receive all my promises. Live out my Words I've spoken through your man of God; believe him, I sent him, and so shall you be established and prosper.

I give you examples in the snow, sleet, sun and rain in all parts of the earth. I give you evidence of my life. I know it like like it's not coming fast enough and you need it now. Have faith, let your patience work perfectly and you shall receive everything in its entirety and you shall not be in want. *This is the Word from God!*

Knowing this, that the trying of your faith worketh patience. But let patience have her perfect work, that ye may be perfect and entire, wanting nothing. (James 1:3-4)

And not only so, but we glory in tribulations also: knowing that tribulation worketh patience; (Romans 5:3)

November 29

What are you doing with your faith? Are you allowing faith to work alone? I ask you these questions because faith doesn't work alone. Faith needs your help. Now you believe all these things I promised you have come to pass; what's your work plan.

You must work while it's day, night comes no man can work. Faith without works is dead being alone. Even the devils believe, but they're working also; seeking whom they might destroy, kill, and steal from.

Faith comes by hearing and hearing the Word from me. In order for faith to come you must hear my Word. In order to receive you must have faith to believe the things you've asked for you will have: Even still you must ask for them.

When you are good, full of my Spirit and faith, much people are added unto me. You must remember without ceasing your work of faith, labor of love, and patience of hope in my son and in my sight, your Father.

I have begun a good work in you and will perform it until the day of Jesus Christ: Knowing this put some work with your faith, don't leave it alone to try and survive on its own; for it will die being alone. *This is the Word from God!*

Even so faith, if it hath not works, is dead, being alone. Yea, a man may say, Thou hast faith, and I have works: shew me thy faith without thy works, and I will shew thee my faith by my works. Thou believest that there is one God; thou doest well: the devils also believe, and tremble. (James 2:17-19)

So then faith cometh by hearing, and hearing by the word of God. (Romans 10:17)

For he was a good man and full of the Holy Ghost and of faith: and much people was added unto the Lord. (Acts 11:24)

Remembering without ceasing your work of faith, and labour of love, an patience of hope in our Lord Jesus Christ, in the sight of God and our Father; (1Thessalonians 1:3)

Being confident of this very thing, that he which hath begun a good work in you will perform it until the day of Jesus Christ: (Philippians 1:6)

And we know that all things work together for the good to them that love God, to them who are the called according to his purpose. (Romans 8:28)

November 30

Scriptures of the Day: Wisdom speaks excellence. Hear; for I will speak of excellent things; and the opening of my lips shall be right things. For my mouth shall speak truth; and wickedness is an abomination to my lips. All words of my mouth are in righteousness; there is nothing forward or perverse in them. They are all plain to him that understandeth, and right to them that find knowledge. Receive my instruction, and not silver; and knowledge rather than choice gold. For wisdom is better than rubies; and all the things that may be desired are not to be compared to it. I wisdom dwell prudence, and find out knowledge of witty inventions. The fear of the Lord is to hate evil: pride, and arrogancy, and the evil way, and the forward mouth, do I hate. Counsel is mine, and sound wisdom: I am understanding; I have strength. I love them that love me; and those that seek me early shall find me. Riches and honour are with me; yea, durable riches and righteousness. That I may cause those that love me to inherit substance; and I will fill their treasures. The Lord possessed me in the beginning of his way, before his works of old. I was set up from everlasting, from the beginning, or ever the earth was. For whoso findeth me findeth life, and shall obtain favour of the Lord. (Proverbs 8:6-14, 17-18, 12-23, 35)

Grace be to you and peace from God our Father, and from the Lord Jesus Christ. Blessed be God, even the Father of our Lord Jesus Christ, the Father of mercies, and the God of all comfort; Who comforteth us in all our tribulation, that we may be able to comfort them which are in any trouble, by the comfort wherewith we ourselves are comforted of God. (2 Corinthians 1:2-4)

Lest Satan should get an advantage of us: for we are not ignorant of his devices. Now thanks be unto God, which always causeth us to triumph in Christ, and maketh manifest the savour of his knowledge by us in every place. (2 Corinthians 2:11, 14)

MONTH OF DECEMBER

December 1

Consider your ways. You have sown much but received little. I've given you grace, peace and mercy. I'm the God of all comfort. I comfort you in tribulation, that you may be able to comfort them that are in any trouble, by the comfort which you are comforted in me, your Father.

Don't allow Satan to trick you with his schemes which I've already made you aware of. I always cause you to win in my son, and have made manifest the known knowledge by you in every place. You have my good Word and comfort in the scriptures.

I've equipped you for the battle; now you have kept the faith, won the fight. Just remember, recognize, realize and receive these testimonies I've given you to build my kingdom and build your house. On this foundation it'll never be destroyed.

Continue to stand strong and step out even when you don't know what you are stepping onto. You are on solid not shaky ground, walk in my perfect will for your life. *This is the Word from God!*

Grace be to you and peace from God our Father, and from the Lord Jesus Christ. Blessed be God, even the Father of our Lord Jesus Christ, the Father of mercies, and the God of all comfort; Who comforteth us in all our tribulation, that we may be able to comfort them which are in any trouble, by the comfort wherewith we ourselves are comforted of God. (2 Corinthians 1:2-4)

Lest Satan should get an advantage of us: for we are not ignorant of his devices. Now thanks be unto God, which always causeth us to triumph in Christ, and maketh manifest the savour of his knowledge by us in every place. (2 Corinthians 2:11, 14)

December 7

Words from God! PIT RIDE: Pain Influenced Through Receiving Information From the Devil and his Empps. What will you ALLOW to HAPPEN? You must choose to *A*lways *L*ive *L*ife *O*beying and *W*anting to *H*ave *A*bundance *P*lenty of *P*eace *E*verlasting *N*ever ending.

December 13

Words from God! L.E.A.P.; Landing Ending Arriving Promises. Leap Land Launch Load; *And he entered into one of the ships, which was Simon's, and* prayed him that he would thrust out a little from *the land. And he sat down, and taught the people out of the ship. Now when he had left speaking, he said unto Simon, Launch out into the deep, and let down your nets for a draught. And Simon answering said unto him, Master, we have toiled all the night, and have taken nothing: nevertheless at thy word I will let down the net. And when they had this done, they enclosed a great multitude of fishes: and their net brake.* (Luke 5:3-6)

DIG BIG (Ending/Beginning) Latter *D*ays *I*s *G*reater; *B*eginning *I*s *G*reater. You must DIG BIG. I shall cause the ending of the year 2011 to be the best ending ever. Expect these last eighteen days to be the best finish of your life.

In order for you to have a great Beginning your finishing must be great. You must allow my great finish to spill over into your great beginning. Your power in praise and power in prayer shall give you all these promotions, provisions, positions and promises; that I have prepared and preserved for you. Remember to give me your most powerful prayer and praise in these last eighteen days and you shall continue to receive my most precious possessions, and prophesies.

Even today I give you an awesome word from me. Listen carefully to me, hear exactly what I am saying, you will never miss it. You are mine, I love you, I chose you in particular, I knew you before I formed you, and I placed and positioned you; because you will pay attention to me. I give you these instructions, follow them to the end.

Watch, pray, praise, and see your blessings manifest in the last days of the year; and never stop manifesting in the beginning of the year, and throughout the year and years to come. You must continue to obey and serve me; and you shall spend your days in prosperity and your years in pleasure. I know this has been a long time coming. The wait is over. It's your time. This Is It. It's my pleasure to prosper you in every area of your life. Receive Now! *This is the Word from God!*

If they obey and serve him, they shall spend their days in prosperity, and their years in pleasures. (Job 36:11)

Let them shout for joy, and be glad, that favour my righteous cause: yea, let them say continually, Let the Lord be magnified, which hath pleasure in the prosperity of his servant. And my tongue shall speak of thy righteousness and of thy praise all the day long. (Psalm 35:27-28)

December 17

IT'S OFFICIAL. Overflow Faith Finances Increase Compassion Inward Anointed Love: I've given you a mouthpiece that even your enemies won't be able to resist. People shall run to you and hear you because of me; and because you have gloried me and not yourself. Continue to hear, listen, speak and do as I command.

You don't have to go looking for me, I'm right her with you, even until the end. I've given you *wisdom, worship* and to be a *witness*. Speak my Word, I've given you; worship the Lord in the beauty of his holiness and be a witness for me. Tell of your testimonies and of my goodness.

When you abide in me and my Words abide in you, you shall ask what you want and it shall be done for you. You have an *overflow* of *faith*; so speak to the mountains, they shall be removed, don't have any doubt in your heart, believe whatever you've spoken, have come to pass and it's yours.

Receive your overflow of *finances* and *increase*. You have *compassion*, and I look at the *inward* man, I've *anointed* you to teach and speak my Word and *love* my people. IT'S OFFICIAL. The ITS have it. This Is It. You're It. It's Done. *This is the Word from God!*

Behold, I have given him for a witness to the people, a leader and commander to the people. Behold, thou shalt call a nation that thou knowest not, and nations that knew not thee shall run unto thee because of the Lord thy God, and for the Holy One of Israel; for he hath glorified thee. Seek ye the Lord while he may be found, call ye upon him while he is near: Let the wicked forsake his way, and the unrighteous man his thoughts: and let him return unto the Lord, and he will have mercy upon him; and to our God, for he will abundantly pardon. So shall my Word be that goeth forth out of my mouth: it shall not return unto me void, but it shall accomplish that which I please, and it shall prosper in the thing whereto I sent it. (Isaiah 55:4-7, 11)

If ye abide in me, and my words abide in you, ye shall ask what ye will, and it shall be done unto you. (John 15:7)

For verily I say unto you, That whosoever shall say, unto this mountain, Be thou removed, and be thou cast into the sea; and shall not doubt in his heart, but shall believe that those things which he saith shall come to pass; he shall have whatsoever he saith. (Mark 11:23)

December 22

Words from God! Done Declared Down Do; I'm your God and your God alone. I formed and created you; I've redeemed and called you in particular and you belong to me. Every place I allow you to go, see and experience whether good or bad; remember I'm with you every step of the way and will never leave your presence.

As you pass through the rivers of waters I'm there and won't allow them to overflow on you. When you walk through the fire you won't be burned or brought to ashes. I'm your Lord, Saviour, and the one and only holy God. Because you are my precious and loved child; I allow you to be honored by men and women I send to your ministry.

Masses of people are coming to Kingdom Minded Church. My kingdom shall reign with people from me for life. You are my witnesses. I chose you to serve me and you know me, and you believe and understand that I'm the one and only true and living God and there will be no other.

I've already Declared, saved and shewed you who I am and always will be. I have sent to the people and brought Down all the good and gracious gifts that you cried out for me to bring into the kingdom and your house. I created this world and I created you; and gave you dominion over everything in it. I will Do a new thing; and how it shall come and happen, it's ok that you don't know yet.

Just know that everyone shall honor you, the good and the bad, the rich and the poor. I make away when you don't even know that there is a way. I provide water upon waters in dry and desert places. I do all these great and wonderful things for you because I made you for myself and for the purpose of shewing forth praise to me. This great glory belongs solely to me. *This is the Word from God!*

But now thus saith the Lord that created thee, O Jacob, and he that formed thee, O Israel, Fear not: for I have redeemed thee, I have called thee by thy name; thou art mine. When thou passest through the waters, I will be with thee; and through the rivers, they shall not overflow thee: when thou walkest through the fire, thou shalt not be burned; neither shall the flame kindle upon thee. For I am the Lord thy God, the Holy One of Israel, thy Saviour; I gave Egypt for thy ransom, Ethiopia and Seba for thee. Since thou wast precious in my sight, thou hast been honourable, and have loved thee: therefore will I give men for thee, and people for thy life. Ye are my witnesses, saith the Lord, and my servant whom I have chosen: that ye may know and believe me, and understand that I am he: before me there was no God formed, neither shall there be after me. I, even I, am the Lord; and besides me there is no savior. I have Declared, and have saved, and I have shewed, when there was no strange god among you: therefore ye are my witnesses, saith the Lord, that I am God. Thus saith the Lord, your redeemer, the Holy One of Israel; For your sake I have sent to Babylon, and have brought Down all their nobles, and the Chaldeans, whose cry is in the ships. Behold, I will Do a new thing; now it shall spring forth; shall ye not know it? I will even make a way in the wilderness, and rivers in the desert. The beast of the field shall honour me, the dragons and the owls: because I give waters in the wilderness, and rivers in the desert, to give drink to my people, my chosen. This people have I formed for myself; they shall shew forth my praise. (Isaiah 43:1-4, 10-14, 19-21)

December 22

ORDER; Obedience Receiving Directions Executing Reign; When you do things in my order, I give you the city. You can go into the enemy's camp and take over. When you Obey, receive my Directions, and Execute my plan you shall Reign forever.

Make sure you do exactly as I say do. Don't add to or take away from my word. My ORDER brings obedience, and overtaking of the opposition. Obedience is key to receiving reigning and remaining.

First thing you must do is take with you people that are ready for war; and people that have been trained. These people are willing because they have accepted and experienced the training; they know how to follow directions. This is my ORDER I give you to receive of my kingdom. *This is the Word from God!*

Let all things be done decently and in order. (1 Corinthians 14:40)

And ye shall compass the city, all ye men of war, and go round about the city once. Thus shalt thou do six days. And seven priests shall bear before the ark seven trumpets of rams' horns: and the seventh day ye shall compass the city seven times, and the priests shall blow with the trumpets. And it shall come to pass, that when they make a long blast with the ram's horn, and when ye hear the sound of the trumpet, all the people shall shout with a great shout; and the wall of the city shall fall down flat, and the people shall ascend up every man straight before him. And it came to pass at the seventh time, when the priests blew with the trumpets Joshua said unto the people, Shout; for the Lord hath given you the city. So the people shouted when the priests blew with the trumpets: and it came to pass, when the people heard the sound of the trumpet, and the people shouted with a great shout, that the wall fell down flat, so that the people went up into the city, every man straight before him, and they took the city. (Joshua 6:3-5, 16, 20)

December 26

What's in your Shopping Cart? Do you have things that you need? Or do you have things that you want? Or do you have both need and want? God says I've supplied all your need according to his riches and glory by Christ Jesus. He will give you the desires or wants; just ask, believe and receive.

God knows what we have need of and he's already supplied your need. You don't have to believe for a need; but you must ask, believe, and receive your want. Remember all your needs are met and you have more of your wants to put into your storehouses or savings.

Your tithes and offerings are for you to have meat in your house. Make sure what we are asking God for is according to his will. Make sure we have a willing heart to obey him in our giving. Give bountifully and be a cheerful giver.

When we place water in our carts, that's a need. He's already given water to the thirsty; rivers of waters (supplied). When we place ice cream in our carts, that's a want. Something we want but don't need. Let's not get caught up with our wants that we forget about your already supplied needs.

Without the need our wants can't we enjoyed. Without the rivers of waters you can't enjoy the boat. The boat needs water and you want to enjoy the ride. You need a house to live in and you want a bed to sleep in comfort. You need transportation and you want a car. You need a job and you want a large paycheck.

Again what are you putting in your shopping cart? Make sure it's love, already provided through giving his son, Jesus Christ. Tithes and offering he's given you a job. Holy Spirit he's given you a helper. Angels he's given them charge over you and they hearken to your voice. A voice to speak his word; A mind to think the things of him; Ears to hear his voice and do, serve, and keep his commandments; and nothing we have need or want will be impossible for us to receive. Make it a good check out! *This is the Word from God!*

But my God shall supply all your need according to his riches in glory by Christ Jesus. (Philippians 4:19)

Therefore I say unto you, What things soever ye desire, when ye pray, believe that ye receive them, and ye shall have them. (Mark 11:24)

But this I say, He which soweth sparingly shall reap also sparingly; and he which soweth bountifully shall reap also bountifully. Every man according as he purposeth in his heart, so let him give; not grudgingly, or of necessity: for God loveth a cheerful giver. And God is able to make all grace abound toward you; that ye, always having all sufficiency in all things, may abound to every good work; (2 Corinthians 9:6-8)

For God so loved the world that he gave his only begotten Son, that whosoever believeth in him should not perish, but have everlasting life. (John 3:16)

Bring ye all the tithes into the storehouse, that there may be meat in mine house; (Malachi 3:10a)

But ye, beloved, building up yourselves on your most holy faith, praying in the Holy Ghost. (Jude 20)

For he shall give his angels charge over thee, to keep thee in all thy ways. (Psalm 91:11)

(As it is written, I have made thee a father of many nations,) before him whom he believed, even God who quickeneth the dead, and calleth those things which be not as though they were. (Romans 4:17)

December 28

I've anointed you to prosper. It's my pleasure to prosper you. You've received your breakthrough favour now! Everything I've promised you is yours now! Live in my manifestations now! The overflow, overtaken, and outpouring of my blessings are in your hands now!

Believe my prophets so shall you prosper. Your thoughts are established in me. Wealth and riches are yours now! You are blessed to be a blessing. You have wisdom from me.

My house is a house of prayer, praise, power, promises, promotions, and provisions. I've revealed my secrets to you through my prophets. You know they are from me because things have already been coming to pass in your life. This is your confirmation. If you haven't received yet just wait its coming; while you're waiting make sure you are doing your part in the process.

My Word shall not return void, it shall accomplish that which I please and prosper whereto I sent it. Trust me, I never lie, I choose who I want to equip and edify me. You must have a willing heart to do my kingdom work.

These last three days of 2011 is the beginning work of the trinity. God the Father, God the Son, and God the Holy Spirit. Pay attention; follow our lead in this order. My son never over steps me and Holy Spirit never over steps him. I make the command, Jesus intercedes, and Holy Spirit reveals the command and you must believe and receive and carry it out.

Continue my process of keeping my commandments, obeying and serving me; you shall always triumph in every situation, circumstances, and area of your life. Always stand with your loins, your (mind) girded, receiving the truth and having righteousness; and your feet shod and (ready) with the preparation of the gospel of peace; Above everything take the shield of faith with you that you shall be able to handle all the fiery darts (thoughts) of the wicked.

Make sure you take your helmet (protection) of salvation, and the sword (Word) of the Spirit, which is the word of God. Always pray your prayer in the Spirit, and watching with perseverance of all saints. Open your mouth and speak boldly and make known the secret of the gospel.

I've given you charge and control. Listen, hear and do what I say. I'm your God, I give you my son Jesus Christ and Holy Spirit to lead, guide, teach, and bring my Word to your remembrance to retain and help you in these last few days of 2011; being your best year ending ever: and all days that's to come. The year 2012 will be the best year beginning and all is well in 2012. *This is the Word from God!*

Stand therefore, having your loins girt about with truth, and having on the breastplate of righteousness; And your feet shod with the preparation of the gospel of peace; Above all, taking the shield of faith, wherewith ye shall be able to quench all the fiery darts of the wicked. And take the helmet of salvation, and the sword of the Spirit, which is the word of God; Praying always with all prayer and supplication in the Spirit, and watching thereunto with all perseverance and supplication for all saints; And for me, that utterance may be given unto me, that I may open my mouth boldly, to make known the mystery of the gospel. (Ephesians 6:14-19)

December 30

I've placed you in high places and positions to complete my work. I've connected you with people in high and top positions to help you in accomplishing the tasks I've given you. You won't know who they are before the work begins because they are already in position before you need them to help you start my work.

Remember what I told you before, I've already supplied your need, I know you need them, that's why I've already placed them there to help you. Follow my instructions and my lead you will never go wrong. I've made you the leader, you shall hear from me first and speak my direction and they shall follow you as I have spoken to them to do so. Do exactly as I say, don't get off *track*, don't *tremble*, *trust* me, you always *triumph* with me.

The enemy will come quickly in your face to suck the life out of you and kill you. Don't be discouraged, I've given you power to defeat him; Use your power in your tongue and choose to live and not die. He can't conquer you; you are more than a conquer through Christ Jesus. Continue to confess my Word, hear me and do as I say; Watch me do a work in you like never before.

Again I say I need you, you need me, they need you and you need them: The people I've placed in position to help you with my work.

People will be envious and jealous, but don't mind them continue on in my work, you'll win if you don't quit.

Again, I've done this work in you and will complete it, until the day of my son, Jesus Christ. You have my reward when you do what I say. I pleased to prosper you in every area of your life; be it Spiritual or natural. I want you to be in health even as your soul prospers. *This is the Word from God!*

And hath raised us up together, and make us sit together in heavenly places in Christ Jesus: (Ephesians 2:6)

He that heareth you heareth me; and he that despiseth you despiseth me; and he that despiseth me despiseth him that sent me. And the seventy returned again with joy, saying, Lord, even the devils are subject unto us through thy name. And he said unto them, I beheld Satan as lightning fall from heaven. Behold, I give unto you power to tread on serpents and scorpions, and over all the power of the enemy: and nothing shall by any means hurt you. Notwithstanding in this rejoice not, that the spirits are subject unto you; but rather rejoice, because your names are written in heaven. All things are delivered to me of my Father; and no man knoweth who the Son is, but the Father; and who the Father is, but the Son, and he to whom the Son will reveal him. And he turned him unto his disciples, and said privately, Blessed are the eyes which see the things that ye see: For I tell you, that many prophets and kings have desired to see those things which ye see, and have not seen them; and to hear those things which ye hear, and have not heard them. (Luke 10:16-20, 22-24)

Beloved, I wish above all things that thou mayest prosper and be in health, even as thy soul prospereth. (3 John 1:2)

Author's Comments

Now you have heard everything I've spoken by my Spirit through my prophet; I didn't reveal these things to you to wonder if it was me speaking to you. You wouldn't have read *T.S.I.T.S. Things Seen In The Spirit* if I wasn't speaking to you. In my speaking month after month, some things have already come to pass; some are happening now, and some will manifest later. Just know what I've spoken to you is real, released, retained, remembered, rendered and received unto you.

To the believer, I know your life has been encouraged, you are excited, expecting greater, and doing greater works for God and the kingdom of God. To the unsaved, you have accepted the greatest gift of all, Jesus Christ. Continue to allow him to be your Lord and Saviour.

Don't be discouraged when trouble times come; they will come but they won't and cannot stay long, they are only temporary. Keep God's commandments, obey and serve him, you will always make it through and triumph in the troubled times.

This is the beginning of the best days and years to come. Thank you for allowing God's Spirit to speak to you through me. Make sure you hear, listen, and do as God has already spoken. Receive his blessings always

Confessions Journal

God's Word spoken in faith, believing, that He will bring it to pass according to His will for our lives.

Introduction

God is so awesome! He has allowed me to hear from Him like never before. As I pray daily and communicate with God and begin to listen to Him; He shares secrets with me to be revealed to the world. First God speaks what He wants to happen, how He wants it done and who He wants to do His work.

For we are his workmanship, created in Christ Jesus unto good works, which God hath before ordained that we should walk in them. God has spoken to me confessions while writing my books Things Seen In The Spirit. He wants the body of Christ and the world that receives Him and His son, Jesus, to receive everything He has promised them. God is so great that He has gives us a word first by His Spirit and through His Prophet. (See Ephesians 2:10)

Surely the Lord God will do nothing, but he revealeth his secret unto his servants the prophets. God has given us a book of confessions to speak daily to assist in bringing everything to pass according to His will for our lives. My prayer is that you continue confessing no matter what situation comes your way. (See Amos 3:7)

If ye continue in the faith grounded and settled, and be not moved away from the hope of the gospel, which ye have heard, and which was preached to every creature which is under heaven; wherefore I Paul am made a minister; I'm writing this book of confessions because God wants us to receive double blessings, dominion over everything and dwell in the land of more than enough. (See Colossians 1:23)

And it shall come to pass, if thou shalt hearken diligently unto the voice of the Lord thy God, to observe and to do all his commandments

Lady Mary Hatter

which I command thee this day, that the Lord thy God will set thee on high above all nations of the earth: And all these blessings shall come on thee, and overtake thee, if thou shalt hearken unto the voice of the Lord thy God. Blessed shalt thou be in the city, and blessed shalt thou be in the field. (See Deuteronomy 28:1-3)

O.F.F.E.R. CONFESSION
Obedience, Faith, Filled, Edifying, Receiving

I am a member of the body of Christ. The church that Jesus built. A body of baptized believers. I am committed to my local church. Sin has no dominion over me. I am free from sin and have become a servant of righteousness. All things are working together for my good, because I love God and are the called according to his purpose. I walk in the Spirit and not the flesh. I am justified by faith; I have peace with God through our Lord, Jesus Christ. I have favor with all people and when I praise God, the Lord added to the church daily and people are saved. I obey the voice of God and the stranger I choose not to follow. I have power to tread over scorpions and serpents.

When I pray I get results, answers, yokes destroyed, have everlasting life, and a relationship with the father, son, and Holy Spirit. Kingdom Minded Church has faithful, committed, dedicated, prompt, honest, loving, tithing, anointed and obedient members. My church has supernatural debt cancellation and supernatural increase and so does my house. The blessings of the Lord have come on and overtaken Kingdom Minded Church members' lives, my life, my family members' lives and all church partners' lives. I have the wisdom, knowledge, and understanding of God's Word now!

Money comes to me now! Money comes to Kingdom Minded Church now! I release angels to hear and carry the Word of God and work for me right now! God has pleasure in my prosperity. I release angels to bring thousands and thousands of members from across the world to Kingdom Minded Church. I release angels to bring forth millions of dollars to my church, my family, church partners, and for myself.

The Lord has sent his angels to watch over me, lest I dash my foot against the stone. I release angels to bring prosperity in my health, my finances, ministry and my marriage. I thank God for his angels working on my behalf.

All members of Kingdom Minded Church have the gift of praying in the Spirit, speaking in tongues, and interpretation of tongues. I sow into good ground and I reap my harvest. I am not a God-robber and there are none in our church.

My body is God's body, it is Holy and I will never put anything evil in God's body. The words that I speak bring grace to the hearers. No filthy, corrupt, communication can come out of my mouth.

I am a doer and not just a hearer of God's Word. I have an ear to hear what the Spirit is saying to the church. I am delivered from the snare of the enemy; Satan has no place in my life, my children's lives, grandchildren's lives or my family members' lives. Because of my righteous intercession, my family is delivered from all evils.

I command every cell, tissue, and blood to flow through my body properly so I can carry out my Kingdom assignment. I pray for all staff needed, any construction, and equipment needed to prosper the Kingdom. I declare increased anointing on my Pastor, my First Lady, my family, my church and my life. I am obedient, I have faith, and I edify the body of Christ. I ask in Jesus name, I believe I have received. Amen.

S.T.E.P. CONFESSION
Saints, Tasting, Enjoyable, Paths

Thank you, Father, for calling me out of darkness into Your marvelous light. God gave me Jesus who suffered for me and left and example; therefore I follow Jesus' steps now and always. Because I'm good, my steps are ordered by the Lord and He delighteth in my ways. I'm not cast down, for the Lord upholdeth me with his hand. Thank God for restoring my soul and leading me in the paths of righteousness for Jesus' sake.

I'm taught in the way of wisdom, God leads me and I walk in right paths. I will never walk into the path of the wicked nor go in the way of evil things or evil people. I enter into peace; I rest in my bed, and always walk in uprightness. The devil doesn't control me; I'm in control.

I submit myself unto God. I resist the devil and he has no place in my life. I'm free from all evils that have held me down. Every move I make and every step I take, God opens the pathway for me to walk in. I always win and I will never be bound by sin.

The law of the Spirit of life in Christ Jesus hath made me free from the law of sin and death. I'm willing and obedient and eating the good of the land. I confess with my mouth the Lord Jesus and believe in my heart that God raised Jesus from the dead, now I'm saved. I ask In Jesus name, I believe, I received. Amen!

FLESH CONFESSION

Flesh, I check you in the name of Jesus! You profit me nothing! You have no good things! Leave now! In the name of Jesus, I command you, Satan, to get thee hence, for it is written and I shall worship the Lord thy God and Him only shall I serve. Satan, you have no place in my life.

Angels are ministering to me now. God has His divine presence in me, therefore I function in His ability. I call those things that are not as though they were and they become. At my command through faith and the Word of God, my family, finances and health are all whole. Any situation that is keeping me from the promises of God I call it gone now! In Jesus' name, amen.

F.O.R.M. CONFESSION
Fishermen Of Real Men

I'm a mighty man of God, strong in the Lord and in the power of His might. I have believing faith and action faith. I walk in the Spirit and not the flesh. Satan doesn't control me; I'm in control. I cast down every evil thought and imagination. I build up and edify the body of Christ. I speak God's word in every situation in my life and for others. The power of God is within me and I release the ability of God's power.

When I pray my prayers are answered and demons tremble at the name of Jesus. I'm the priest, provider, and protector of my home. Because I'm righteous, my family is blessed and no evil can befall them. Jesus is the author and finisher of my faith.

I love my wife as my own body. I love my wife as Christ also loved the Church and gave himself for it. I'm kept from the evil woman, from the flattery of the tongue of a strange woman. I have unconditional love for my wife; I trust her and do no evil against her. I have no iniquities or sins; therefore no good things are withheld from me.

What I understand no one can take away from me. I don't look back, I press toward the mark for the prize of the high calling of God in Christ Jesus. This mind is in me, which is also in Christ Jesus. I keep my mind stayed on Jesus and He keeps me in perfect peace, a peace which passeth all understanding.

I witness to the lost and they are saved. I submit myself to God, I resist the devil and he has no place in my life. I have a mind to work and a faith that works. I speak to mountains, they are removed and casted into the sea, I have no doubt in my heart, I believe what I say has come to pass, and I have whatsoever I say. I ask all things in Jesus' name, believing that I have already received them. Amen.

GOD'S C.H.A.S.E.D. WOMEN CONFESSION

I'm a virtuous woman, my family calls me blessed. I speak with wisdom and faith instruction is on my tongue. I take care of my household. I obey God and he rewards me for my works. I have believing faith and action faith. I'm filled with the Holy Spirit and I speak with other tongues as God gives me the utterance. The words that I speak bring grace to the hearers; no filthy corrupt communication can come out of my mouth.

I seek first the kingdom of God and His righteousness and all these things are added unto me. When I Pray I get Results, Answers, Yokes destroyed, have Everlasting life, and a Relationship with the Father, Son and Holy Spirit. As a God Chased Woman, I'm Christ Centered in my Confession. The Holy Spirit is Housed in my Heart. I am Accountable Always for my Actions. I'm Saved, Sanctified in my Soul. I have Everlasting Evidence in my Example. I'm Determined, Delivered from my fleshly Desires.

I have an ear to hear what the Spirit is saying to me. I'm a doer and not just a hearer of God's Word. I'm blessed going in and blessed coming out. The words I speak bring life and not death. I'm spiritually minded and I have life and peace. My husband loves me unconditionally, he praises me, he's faithful to me, he's trustworthy, he never lies to me, and he's righteous and a God fearing man. Because I fear the Lord, I'm praised. I do my husband good and not evil all the days of my life. My husband trusts me, and does me good and not evil every day of his life.

I'm willing and obedient and eating the good of the land. I stretch out my hands to the poor; I reach forth my hands to the needy. Thank God for his Word which says: "So shall my word be that goeth forth out of my mouth: it shall not return unto me void, but it shall accomplish that which I please, and it shall prosper in the thing where to I sent it." Therefore, I speak God's word in every situation in life for myself and for others. I obey God's word, I ask in Jesus' name, I believe and I received. Amen!

KEEPING KNOWN KNOWLEDGE
CONTROLLING THE TONGUE AND MOUTH

Father, I thank you that I have a wholesome tongue and it is a tree of life. I choose to use my tongue for speaking good and not evil, because Your Word says, perverseness of the tongue therein is a breach in the Spirit; I speak life and not death with the power of my tongue and receive the good fruit thereof.

Thank you, Father, that I keep my mouth and tongue and my soul is kept from troubles. I open my mouth with wisdom and my tongue is the law of kindness. Father, I thank You that I am the just and my tongue is as choice silver.

God, I thank You for giving me wisdom to lay up knowledge and my mouth is not foolish or near destruction. I call those things that are not as thou they were and they become. Any situation or spoken words that are keeping me from walking in the promises of God, I call it gone now! Thank you, God, I keep my mouth and my life. In Jesus name I believe, I received. Amen!

A PRAYER FOR SALVATION ON BEHALF OF OTHERS

Father, I come before You in prayer and in faith, believing, Your Word, which says that You desire all men to be saved and come into the knowledge of the truth, so I bring (person you're praying for) before You this day.

I break the power of Satan from his assignments and activities in (person you're praying for) life in the name of Jesus. Now, while Satan is bound, I ask that You send forth the perfect laborers to share the good news of the gospel in such a way that he/she will listen and understand it. As the truth is ministered, I believe (person you're praying for) will come to his/her senses and come out of the snare of the devil and make Jesus the Lord of his/her life.

Father, I ask that You fill (person you're praying for) with the knowledge of your will in all wisdom and Spiritual understanding. As I intercede on his/her behalf, I believe that the power of Holy Spirit is activated and from this moment on, I shall praise and thank You for (person you're praying for)'s salvation. I am confident that You are alert and active, watching over Your Word to perform it. It will not return to you void. It will accomplish that which You please, and prosper in the thing whereto it was sent.

Therefore, my confession of faith is, "God has begun a good work in (person you're praying for)'s life and he will perform it and bring it to full completion until the day of Jesus Christ, in Jesus' name. Amen.

Scripture references from the amplified bible:
2 Peter 3:9; Matthew 18:18, 9:37-38; 2 Timothy 2:26; Jeremiah 1:12.

GIVING PRAISE AND THANKS TO GOD

I will praise thee, O Lord, with my whole heart. I will shew forth all thy marvelous works. I will be glad and rejoice in thee. I will sing praises to thy name, O thou most high. Give unto the Lord the glory due unto his name; worship the Lord in the beauty of his holiness.

I will bless the Lord at all times and his praise shall continually be in my mouth. My soul shall make her boast in the Lord, the humble shall hear thereof, and be glad. O, magnify the Lord with me and let us exalt his name together. I will give thee thanks in the great congregation; I will praise thee among much people.

My tongue shall speak of righteousness and of thy praise all the daylong. I will greatly fear my God in the assembly of the saints, and I will reverence him along with all of them that are about him. Thank you, God, for blessing me to know the joyful sound. Thank you, God, for allowing me to rejoice all the day, and in thy righteousness You have exalted me. Because Your Word says: it's a good thing to give thanks unto the Lord and to sing praises unto Thy name O most high, I give You praise now!

I'm planted in the house of the Lord and flourishing in the courts of my God. Lord I give unto You the glory due Your name. I shall bring an offering, and come unto Your courts. Oh, how I worship You, Lord, in the beauty of Your holiness. I make a joyful noise unto You, Lord. I serve You, Lord, with gladness; and I come before Your presence with singing.

I know that You are my Lord and my God. Thank you, God, for making me and not allowing me to have anything to do with it. I'm Your child and the sheep of Your pasture. I enter into Your gates with thanksgiving, and unto Your courts with praise, I'm thankful unto You, as I bless Your name. For You, Lord, are good, Your mercy is everlasting, and Your truth endureth to all generations.

Thank you, Lord, for my total being and always being there with me. In Jesus' name. Amen!

DELIVERANCE PRAYER

Lord, I pray that You would strengthen me to resist any temptation that comes my way, removes it out of my mind before it ever reaches my heart or personal experience. Lead me not into temptation but deliver me from evils such as (whatever evils you are praying about). Remove temptation especially in the area of (whatever deliverance). Make me strong where I'm weak. Help me to rise above anything that erects itself as a strong hold in my life.

Psalms 101:3 says: I will set nothing wicked before my eyes; I hate the work of those who fall away; it shall not cling to me.

Lord, You've said that whoever has no rule over his own Spirit is like a city broken down, without walls. (Proverbs 25:28)

I pray that I will not be broken down by the power of evil, but raised up by the power of God. Establish a wall of protection around me. Fill me with Your Spirit and flush out all that is not of You. Lord, help me to abhor that which is evil; and cling to that which is good. (Romans 12:9)

I pray that I will be repulsed by tempting situations. Give me courage to reject them. Teach me to walk in the Spirit so I will not fulfill the lust of the flesh. Lord, You have said to call upon You in the day of trouble and You will deliver us. (Psalms 50:15)

I call upon You now and ask that You would work deliverance in my life, deliver me from anything that binds me set me free from (whatever deliverance). Deliver me quickly and be a rock of refuse and a fortress of defense to save me. (Psalms 31:2)

Lift me away from the hands of the enemy. (Psalms 31:15)

Bring me to a place of understanding where I can recognize the work of evil and cry out to You for help. If the deliverance I pray for is not immediate, keep me from discouragement and help me to be confident that You have begun a good work in me and will complete it. (Philippians 1:6)

Give me the certainty that even in my most hopeless state, when I find it impossible to change anything You, Lord, can change everything. Help me understand that we do not wrestle against flesh and blood, but against principalities, against powers, against the rulers of darkness of this age, and spiritual wickedness in high places. (Ephesians 6: 12)

Things Seen in the Spirit

I pray that I will be strong in the Lord and in the power of his might and put on the whole armor of God, so I can stand against the wiles of the devil in the evil day.

Mediate these scriptures:
Ephesians 6:13-18; Psalms 18: 2, 3; Psalms 91:14; Psalms 18:16-19; Psalms 56: 13; Luke 4:18

The Spirit of the Lord is upon me, because he has anointed me to preach the gospel to the poor; he has sent me to heal the broken hearted, to proclaim deliverance to the captives and recover of sight to the blind, to set a liberty those who are oppressed.

PRAYER TO BE FILLED WITH THE HOLY SPIRIT
My heavenly Father, I am a believer. I am Your child and You are my Father. Jesus is my Lord. I believe with all my heart that Your Word is true. Your Word says that, if I will ask, I will receive Holy Spirit, so in the name of Jesus Christ, my Lord, I am asking You to fill me to overflowing with Your precious Holy Spirit. Baptize me in Your Holy Spirit.

Because of your Word, I believe that I now receive and I thank you for Your Holy Spirit. I believe that Holy Spirit is within me and, by faith, I accept him. Now, Holy Spirit, rise up within me as I praise my God. I fully expect to speak with other tongues, as You give me the utterance.

Meditate These Scriptures on the Holy Spirit:
John 14:10, 12, 16-17; Acts 1:8, 2:4,32-33, 39, 8:12-17, 10:44-46, 19:2, 5-6; 1 Corinthians 14:2-15, 18, 27; Ephesians 6:18; Jude 20.

R.E.A.C.H. CONFESSION
Revelation, Everlasting, Anointing, Compassion, Holy Spirit

I'm girding up the loins of my mind; I'm sober and hoping to the end, for the grace that is to be brought unto me, at the revelation of Jesus Christ. I have no fear because it's my Father's good pleasure to give me the Kingdom. Thank you, God, for revelation knowledge.

God's Kingdom is everlasting and his dominion endureth throughout all generations. I have dominion over everything upon the earth. Thank you, God, for the anointing flowing freely upon me. I have the same compassion as Jesus. Holy Spirit leads guides and teaches me; therefore I observe all things and remember everything God has spoken to me.

God speaks harvest; I receive it. Holy Spirit gives revelation; I receive it. God anoints my head with oil; I receive it. My cup runs over and overflows now! The blessings of the Lord are overtaking me now! I'm full of revelation and it's everlasting.

Thank God for the anointing, the compassion and Holy Spirit being my helper. Everything God has promised me is within reach. I reach and receive now! In Jesus' name. Amen.

S.H.O.W. CONFESSION
Seedtime, Harvest-Time, Overflowing, Wealth

My harvest is plenteous and I'm one of the few laborers that God sends forth into his harvest. I freely receive and I freely give. When I give it is given unto me with good measure, pressed down, shaken together and running over and men have given unto my bosom. I lift up my eyes and look on the fields; they are white already to harvest. I'm a breeder of abundance.

Angels have keeping power and charge over me. God has given me seedtime and harvest time. Thank God for my fruit, multiplying and remaining. I receive all that God has for me and nothing and no one can stop my overflow. I'm living in the promises of God and my life will never be the same from this day forward. I'm walking in abundance, my children are walking in abundance, and my family, friends and church are all walking in abundance. I will never turn back.

Thank you, God, for giving me this overflow, harvest, abundance and wealth. The windows of heaven's blessings are overflowing in my life now! I'm the just and the wealth of the wicked is mine now! God is my source and God is my supplier.

Seedtime is always harvest time for my financial future. I'll never be broke another day in my life. Thank God for his love and blessings to all mankind. In Jesus' name. Amen!

LOVE CONFESSION

Father, in Jesus' name, I thank You that I am walking in love. God, because you are love, I have the power of love on the inside of me. Thank you, Holy Ghost, for You have poured love in my heart. I have not the Spirit of fear, but of power, and of love, and of a sound mind.

Thank God for my faith, wisdom, knowledge, understanding and most importantly my love. Love overflows in my life always. My love gives me power and ability to get wealth. I prosper because I love God. I give because I love God. I love You, God, and I thank You for giving me what I ask.

I am dwelling in the secret place of the most high and abiding under the shadow of the almighty. Lord, You are my refuge and my fortress, and in you, God, I do trust. I walk in the presence of God; therefore I receive His fullness, His anointing, His peace, His blessings, His love, His mercy, His grace and His Holy Spirit.

Love never fails. Even though I have faith and hope abiding in me, love is the greatest. I thank you, God, for giving me the greatest love of all, Your son, Jesus. I call love into the hearts of all mankind now, in Jesus' name. Amen.

H.E.A.L.I.N.G. CONFESSION
Holy Spirit, Entering, Abiding, Living, Inside, The Godly

Father God, I thank You for taking the taste for (whatever healing) out of my mouth and the desire for (whatever healing) out of my heart. Father, Your Word says that You wish above all things that I prosper and be in health, even as my soul prospereth. I thank you, God, for my good health now.

God, I thank You for Jesus, and when I call His name, Jesus! Jesus! Jesus! Something happens right now! Father, thank you for healing and deliverance right now! You have delivered me from (whatever healing) and healed me from (whatever healing) I call those things that are not as though they were and they become right now! Every organ, tissue, muscle, nerve, and cell of my body functions in perfection and lines up with the Word of God and I live to carry out my Kingdom assignment.

I thank you, Father, for the blood flowing properly in my body. Father, because I diligently hearken to Your voice, I do what's right in Your sight and keep Your commandments, therefore no sickness or disease can destroy me. I call healing in my body now! I thank you, God, for being my healer.

Thank you, God, for making me a hearer and doer of Your Word, therefore I have life and health in my body. Father, I thank You for sending Your Word and healing and delivering me from (whatever healing) now! I believe. I've received in Jesus' name. Amen!

PEACE CONFESSION

Thank you, Father, for keeping me in perfect peace and keeping my mind stayed on you. I have peace that surpasses all my understanding. Your Word says that to everything there is a season and a time to every purpose under the heaven: Father, I thank you for my time of peace every day of my life. I praise You, God, and give You glory in the highest.

Thank you for my peace and good will towards all mankind. Thank you, God, for Jesus. I thank you, Father, that my heart isn't troubled or afraid. Even though bad things come in my life, I thank you, God, that You said I will have peace. I thank you, God, for my peace with You through Jesus Christ.

I thank you, God, for Your peace that rules in my heart; which You have called in my body. I obey Your Word that says follow peace with all men and holiness, without which no man shall see the Lord. I will not let my peace be disturbed or cause anyone else peace to be disturbed. In Jesus' name. Amen.

PRAISE TO GOD BRINGS T.H.I.S.
Trust Help Increase Safety

I trust in You, Lord; You are my help and shield. Thank you, Lord, for being mindful of me, blessing my house and the house of others. You bless those that fear you, both small and great. God, I thank you for my increase. I'm blessed of You, Lord, which made heaven and earth. The heaven, even the heavens are Yours, Lord; but the earth you have given to us. Thank you, God, for this earth and allowing us to dwell in Your fullness on this earth.

I called upon You, Lord, in distress; You answered me and set me in a large place. Thank you, Lord, for being on my side. I will not fear, because man can't hurt me, as long as You are with me. Thank you, God, for taking my part with them that help me; therefore shall I see my desire upon them that hate me. God, I thank You for my safety. For in the time of trouble, You shall hide me in Your pavilion; in the secret of Your tabernacle shall You hide and place me upon a rock.

I thank you, God, for lifting my head above mine enemies 'round about me. I'm not dead, therefore I will praise You and never be silent in praising You. I will continue to praise You from this time forth and for evermore.

THANKSGIVING CONFESSION

Father, I thank You for everything at all times. For this is Your will, in Christ Jesus concerning me. I come before Your presence, God, with thanksgiving and I make a joyful noise unto You with praise. God, I give you thanks before all people and I speak of all Your wonderful works. Father, thank you for creating the fruit of my lips; thank you, God, for peace — peace to them that are far off, and to them that are near. God, thank you for bringing us all back to You.

Father, Your Word says, for whatsoever is born of God overcometh the world: and this is the victory that overcometh the world, even our faith. I thank You, Father, for giving me life and life more abundantly; and making me more than a conqueror through Jesus Christ. God, thank you for the blessings of Abraham that have come on us through Jesus Christ and we receive the promise of Your Spirit through faith.

Thank you for pouring out Your Spirit on us, and revealing all things to us by Your spirit. Thank you, Father, for giving us confidence to ask anything according to Your will and You hear us. God, thank you for hearing us and giving us what we ask of You.

God, we believe in You and we are established; we believe Your prophets and we prosper. Because of our praise and thanksgiving, You set ambushments against our enemies and destroyed them. Father, we thank You for mercy, grace, favor, and your goodness toward us.

Thank you, God, for forced, focused, and faithful thanksgiving we give to You. We saturate ourselves in prayer, praise and power of thanksgiving always. We use our voice of thanksgiving as a weapon for You to get involved and move on our behalf. Thank you, Father, for effectiveness and expression of thanksgiving.

L.I.F.E. CONFESSION
Live In Faith Everyday

I live to love and I love to live. I'm in this world, but this world is not in me. I have Faith in God and God is faithful to me. Everyday is a day to give thanks to God, and everyday I give God thanks for everything he has preserved, promised, and provided to me. All of my burdens are removed; yokes are destroyed.

I'm living this life, and life is worth living. I receive brand new mercies everyday and a mighty move of God everyday. I'm living in the manifestations of everything I've asked according to God's will everyday. I never go a day without being in God's presence and speaking, hearing, doing and listening to Him.

In this Life, I have love, joy, peace, longsuffering, gentleness, goodness, faith, meekness, and temperance. In this life, I'm crucified with Christ: nevertheless I live; yet not I, but Christ liveth in me: and the life which I live in the flesh I live by the faith of the Son of God, who loved me, and gave himself for me. I can continue to live to love and love to live in this world by faith every day. Thank you, God, for being in Christ Jesus. Amen!

B.L.E.S.S.I.N.G. CONFESSION
Believing Living Everyday Sufficient Surplus Increase Never lacking Giving

I hearken diligently unto the voice of the Lord my God. I observe and do all His commandments, which He has commanded me this day. The Lord has set me high above all nations of the earth. All these blessings have come on me and overtaken me. I receive my on-time reservation of blessings right now!

God, You are the greatest and I always expect the great. I'm blessed in the city and blessed in the field. Thank you, God, for opening unto me Your good treasure. God, I thank You for the heavens giving the rain unto my land in my season. Thank you, Lord, for blessing the work of my hand, which, makes me a lender and not a borrower. I obey and serve You, God; therefore I spend my days in prosperity and my years in pleasure.

Thank you, God, for having pleasure in prospering me. Father, thank you that You wish above all things that I prosper and be in health, even as my soul prospereth. God, thank you for blessing me over and over again. God's blessings make me rich and add no sorrow. I have the not enough room to receive blessings. I choose the blessings and I'm always receiving blessings. In Jesus' name. Amen.

M.I.N.D. CONFESSION
Marvelous Imagination Never Doubting

I cast down every evil thought and imagination that's not like You, God. I replace and receive all thoughts that are true, honest, pure, just, lovely and of good report, and have virtue. My mind is alert, aware, and I'm not alarmed by any tricks, or traps of Satan. I have a pure heart. God has created in me a clean heart and renewed the right spirit within me.

God is my source, sustainer, and supplier of my sound mind and I serve Him only. Satan, you are a liar and I will never trust you. I submit myself unto God and I resist the devil in the name of Jesus. I call those things that are not as though they were and they become. Any situation or circumstance that are not of God, I call gone now in Jesus' name.

I'm precious in God's sight, He loves me and I'm His friend. Because I'm God's friend He lays down His life for me. I know God is for me and no one in this world can be against me. I have hope, I'm happy, I'm honored, and I'm healed. I'm delivered from everything and everyone that has tried or did hurt me. All people love me and I love them. I put away all distractions and disturbance that try to destroy me. I'm blessed going in and blessed coming out. I have peace that surpasses all understanding. God keeps me in perfect peace and my mind is stayed on Him.

Holy Spirit leads, guides, and teaches me; and brings all things to my remembrance that God speaks and has spoken to me. I trust Holy Spirit always and I call on him daily. God has given me, wisdom, knowledge and understanding of His Word. I have the wisdom, Word and wealth of God always. I'm strong in the Lord and in the power of His might. I believe I've received all God has for me Now and forever. In Jesus' name. Amen.

S.H.A.P.E. CONFESSION
Saving Healing Attack Provide Elevate

Father I thank You for saving me as I confess with my mouth the Lord Jesus and believe in my heart that You, God, raised him from the dead as Your Word tells me in Romans 10:9, 13. God, I thank You for Your Word in Isaiah 53:5. I choose to believe Your report, Father, which says Jesus was wounded for my transgressions, He was bruised for my iniquities: the chastisement of my peace was upon Him and with His stripes I'm healed. I believe I have received my healing now! In Jesus' name.

God, I praise You and You fight my battles and my enemies are defeated. According to Your Word in 2 Chronicles 20:22. I don't have to worry about my enemies; I continue to praise You through it all. Thank you, Father, for making me the lender and not the borrower. You provide for your lenders according to Luke 6:38.

When I give it is given unto to me, with good measure, pressed down, shaken together and running over, shall men give unto my bosom. I shall continue to sow my seeds and meet the needs of the people that you have set apart to receive. As Your Word says in Ephesians 2:10: I'm Your workmanship, created in Christ Jesus to do good works, which you God hath before ordained that I should walk in them. Thank you, Father, for allowing me to be in SHAPE NOW! In Jesus' name. Amen.

L.E.A.P. CONFESSION
Lifting Encouraging Always Praising

Father, I thank You that the earth is Yours and the fullness thereof, the world and they that dwell therein. I lift up my head and I'm lifted up. Thank you, Father, for being my King of glory and coming into my life. Father, I thank You for being strong and mighty and mighty in battle.

God, You are my light and my salvation and I shall not fear. Thank you, God, for being the strength of my life and I don't have any fear; when the wicked even my enemies and my foes try to come against me to destroy they fell. I bless You, Lord, at all times and Your praise shall continually be in my mouth. I magnify You, Lord, and I exalt Your name. Thank you, God, for delivering me from my enemies and all my fears.

O taste and see that the Lord is good. I thank you, Lord, and I trust You. I shout unto You, God, with the voice of triumph. Father, thank you for arising and my enemies are scattered. I sing praises to You, God, and give You thanks, O most high.

I make a joyful noise unto you, Lord, with all the people. I serve You, Lord, with gladness and come before You with praises and thanksgiving. Father, thank You for daily loading me with benefits, which I will not forget that You gave them to me.

I praise You in the sanctuary; I praise You for your awesome presence and power. I praise You for your mighty acts. I praise You for your excellence and greatness. I praise You with loud sounding instruments and with a dance. With all that I am and all that I do and every breathe that I take, I give You praise. In Jesus' name. Amen!

(RENEWED) M.I.N.D. CONFESSION
Meditating Imaging Nothing Damaging

Thank you, Father, for keeping my mind stayed on You and You keeping me in perfect peace — this peace that surpasses all understanding. My mind is alert, my mind is clear. I think things that are true, honest, just, pure, lovely and good report. I control my thoughts the devil don't control them. I cast down every and all thoughts or imaginings not of you God. Father, thank you that I don't allow anyone or anything to stop me from hearing, listening, and doing what You have called, commissioned, and commanded me to do. I follow and know the voice of Holy Spirit.

Thank you, God, that my husband never lies to me. He loves me unconditionally. He desires me only. He's honest and trustworthy. Holy Spirit reveals all things to me by His Spirit. I hear Your voice, God, and not the deceiver or stranger. Father, thank you for I obey You and do what You say at all times.

God, thank you that my thoughts are the thoughts You want me to have. I meditate on Your Word day and night. I submit myself unto You, Lord. I resist the devil and he flees from me. Father, thank you that the devil can't destroy me with damaging words or thoughts. The hurts I have experienced in the past or the hurts that try to come against me now will not affect me now or ever. Thank you for giving me an awesome mind.

Every thought from Holy Spirit; I embrace them, I live by them and I receive them daily. Father, thank you for giving me dominion and control over everything including my mind. I receive every good and perfect gift from you now! In Jesus' name. Amen!

W.O.R.S.H.I.P. CONFESSION
Wiliness Outpouring Releasing Soul Having Inward Praise

Lord, I love You and I worship You with all my heart, and with all my soul, and with all my might. I keep Your Words You command this day in my heart always. Thank you, God, for being the one and only Lord of my life. God, I thank You and I give You Glory and Honor in your Presence.

Thank you, Lord, for Your strength and gladness in this Your holy place. I worship You, Lord, in the beauty of Your holiness. I come to You, Lord, with everything that I am and everything that I have. I give it all back to You, Father. God, I use my mind, body, and soul for Your kingdom work and Your pleasure.

Thank you, God, as I worship You, Your glory, Your honor, Your strength, Your gladness and Your love is revealed in me. Lord, I worship You for giving me Your Son, Jesus. Now, Jesus, I give You permission to sit in my disappointments, and distractions and everything that tries to devastate or destroy me. Thank you, Jesus, I follow Your example now and always.

God, I worship You in Spirit and in truth. Thank you, for I know the truth and the truth have made me free. God, I rejoice and I am glad along with the heavens and the earth. Lord, You reigneth; and we receive of all Your goodness, Your grace, and Your glory. Lord, let all the earth speak of Your goodness and let Your mercy endureth forever. We worship You, Lord, as You have delivered us from the heathens and now they are our inheritance.

God, as we worship You in our praise; You add souls from the north, south, east and west, to be a part of Your kingdom daily; such as to be saved. Thank you, God, for increasing our church, our ministries, marriage and our homes.

Thank you, God, for loving us so that You gave us the love of Your life: Your Son, Jesus. We believe in Jesus, therefore we won't perish but have everlasting life. Thank you, Father, for being Lord over our lives and being the joy of our salvation. We give You glory in our praise; as we worship You ,God, now and always. In Jesus' name. Amen!

BLOOD APPLIED CONFESSION

Father, I thank You for my Blood Applied State. I thank You for staying Released as I have been Remodeled and Remade through the blood of Your Son, Jesus Christ, who gave Himself as a sacrifice for us. Father, I thank you for the blood of Jesus has purified my mind of all dead works as I have chosen to serve You. Thank you, Father, for my thoughts are true honest just pure lovely and of good report.

God, I thank You for Your Word in John 14:21; which says, He that hath my commandments, and keepeth them, he it is that loveth me: and he that loveth me shall be loved of my Father, and I will love him, and will manifest myself to him. Father I love you and your son, Jesus Christ. I have and shall keep your commandments, and always do what you tell me to do: therefore you will constantly and continue to manifest yourself to me.

I have the mind of Jesus Christ because of the blood that was shed for me at the cross. Father, I thank You that I'm Redeemed Reconciled and Restored back to You through the blood of Jesus and the cross experience. Thank you, Father, for my sins have been forgiven through the blood of Jesus, therefore my feet are not swift to shed blood and your blood is on me my children and grandchildren.

God, I thank you that no plague shall come upon me and destroy me because the blood of Jesus has been Applied on the doors of my house and the plague passes over it. Father God, I thank You that I'm never far away from You because the blood has brought me close to You. Father, I confess and receive Your Word in John 6:56 which says, I feed on your flesh drink your blood as I dwell continually in You and You dwell continually in me.

Father, thank you for allowing the blood to seal the covenant which you commanded [me to deliver to You. Father God, I thank You that I now have full freedom and confidence to enter into the Holy of Holies by the power, authority, strength, virtue, and moral excellence of grace through the blood of Jesus Christ. Father, I thank You that because of the blood that has been applied, I am blessed, You have enlarged my borders, Your hand is with me, You have kept me from all evils and nothing shall ever hurt me.

Father God, thank you that Your will has been done in my life. I believe I have received. In Jesus' name. Amen.

PROSPERITY CONFESSION

My hands are anointed to prosper everything that my hands touches prospers. I have the money cometh anointing on me. God has made it this way and its here to stay. My blessings are on the way. Angels are moving my way today.

Open the doors open the mail, checks are here, and checks are revealed and received. I use my money wisely. I didn't give up I kept the faith, that's why money is on the way. I have more money in my hands that I could have ever imagined.

I've slowed down and I won't miss a minute or a moment of my manifestations, which have come divinely directed, and delivered to me NOW!!! God has caused men for the vision and people for my life to prosper me, even my soul prospers. Men are giving unto my bosom. God has released my promises, promotions, and prosperity NOW!!! In Jesus' name.

Today and every day shall be a great calling and coming in of money, that I didn't know was coming, and money that I did know was coming. I'm reaping where I haven't sown, because of the unknown, and the all knowing, sufficient surplus, and supernatural things from my almighty, all-powerful God. He has caused this increase.

I believe in God and my thoughts are established. I believe His prophets, so am I prospering. It's never a coincidence in God. What I have called has come. The millions of dollars have come and shall never stop coming, as I never stop sowing. I'm the seed of Abraham and as his seed I'm prospering, and bare much fruit; and it's multiplied, manifested, mounted, and magnetically drawn to me NOW!!!

Money never is detaching always attaching, attracting, and attacking me forever. I continue in Gods Spirit by praying in the Holy Spirit; which reveals to me how to continue to receive Gods wealth and riches, that's already been placed in my house. God have cause people to sow more than what they planed on sowing into your life.

My bank account prospers. My mind prospers. My heart prospers. My creative ideas and witty inventions prosper. My marriage prospers. My ministries prosper. My health prospers. UPE Designs prospers. My new houses and home prospers. My new lands and new properties prosper. My new trucks and cars prosper. My children and grand baby prosper. Everything my hand touches prospers.

I always say what I want and desire, and it lines up with God's Word. I reach out it's there for my receiving. I receive NOW and I Enjoy!!! Thank You, Jesus!

M.O.N.E.Y. CONFESSION
Manifestation Overflowing Navigating Every Year

I am married to money. I have money to pay my vows. I have mountains of money. Money is mounted manifesting and moving into my hands now. I receive my money now. I use my money wisely. Angels are loaded down with my money and bringing it to me now. I have mansions houses and land.

I sow my seed in good soil and the white fields are already harvested. I have an overflow outpouring and overtaking of money that harvesting and coming to me now. My money has growth it continues to grow and never stops growing. When I sow, I target my money for the harvest. This process has brought me my continual harvest.

I have wisdom money. Money goes where I tell it to go. I obey God and I take my money to its destination. My money can't be derailed or destroyed because it's always on track. My money is determined destined and delivered to me now. My money is blessed and bountiful and always working for me. I am the manager and master of my money.

Money does what I tell it to do. Money has changed my life for the better. Money always works for my good. My money isn't poor, it has purpose procedure it provides and prospers me. I am a moneymaker. Money is my servant, and it serves the purpose of which I obtained it for.

Money builds God's kingdom first and then it builds my house. I never lose my money. I have a plan for my money and I work the process, which causes me to continue living in wealth and riches which has already been provided in my house. In Jesus' name. Amen.

WEALTH CONFESSION
Wholeness Exceedingly Abundantly Loaded True Harvest

Thank you, God, for wealth and riches being in my house. Father, I thank You for making me a God-made millionaire. Thank you, God, for making me prosper. I am blessed in the cities and blessed in the fields. I have dominion I am subduing replenishing and multiplying. I have channels of wealth to flow through, and I am a channel of wealth for people to flow through. Thank you, God, for pouring out Your wealth and riches to me.

I bless those who You have set apart from the rest for me to bless. Thank you, God, for allowing me to stay faithful in the lean times now I am financially full in my times and seasons of harvest. Father, I thank You for choosing me to be one of Your few laborers in this plenteous harvest.

God I thank You for allowing the people to know that I am a God-made miracle millionaire. I call money to me now. Money cometh to me today and every day. Money never stops coming to me.

I am willing and obedient and eating the good of the land I obey and serve God therefore I spend my days in prosperity and my years in pleasure. I believe God's prophets so I am prospering. God, I thank You for Your power resting on me.

I have witty inventions and creative ideas on the inside of me and they are coming out now. I have the mind of Christ Jesus. God I thank You for blessing me with whatever I set my mind to do that's according to Your will and word. I ask of You, God, in the spirit realm and

I believe and confess it in the natural realm therefore You, God, have made it manifest to me in the natural realm.

God, I thank You for allowing my big dreams to become visible to me now. I am living the life God made and called me to live. Father, thank you for my time and seasons of increase. Increase is in my house now and always. Father God, thank you, for You have made me ready and ripe to receive my harvest.

I will never waste my wealth, because I abide in You and Your words abide in me I have asked for an abundance of money to come to me and You have made money to manifest to me now in Jesus' name, amen.

MARRIAGE CONFESSION
Motivated Always Reaching Receiving Increasing And Great Example

Father, thank you for our marriage, it is full of love and honesty. There will no adultery, lies or mistrust in our marriage. We obey and follow Your plan for our marriage. Thank you, God, for what You put together no one can separate. We have done what You said; which is leave father and mother and cleave to each other.

Father, thank you for allowing us to love each other unconditionally as we love You unconditionally. We never forget to pray every day for each other and pray together. Thank you, God, for helping us to stay in agreement always, as You will never withhold anything from us. We continue to be on one according speaking the same language and there is nothing we can ever imagine to do that You won't do for us.

Father God, thank you for allowing Your Holy Spirit to bring to our remembrance every spoken Word, way and wisdom on how to be and stay married. Thank you, God, for Your Holy Spirit teaching, leading and guiding us in every way. Thank you, God, for showing us how to love each other and love being our motivation in this marriage as it is for You. Thank you, God, for giving us a heart for each other.

We are up on the inside of each other's hearts. Our hearts are open to love and have compassion for each other. There's trust for each other and truths told to each other. Wrong is recognized and revealed, and we have wisdom and God Word is obeyed and received. Our hearts are clean and clear of clog, confusion, corruption, and shall continue in correction. No other male or female can interrupt our hearts for each other.

Everything not from God has been evicted from our hearts, and nothing wrong can enter in. Thank you, God, for always being in our hearts, as Your spirit of truth resides in us. Holy Spirit helps us to always recognize that the power of God rests, rule, resonate, reign, and remain is in our hearts forever. We always believe and receive what God sees, says, and speaks to our hearts.

Father, thank you that we never receive anything or anyone into our hearts that You didn't give us. Love is spread abroad in our hearts and it will never depart because we are set apart. God, thank You for our marriage is and always will be what You called, chose, commanded, and commissioned it for, and You will continue to give us more and more as You open doors.

We receive Your overflowing and outpouring of bountiful blessings in our marriage forever and we are forever grateful. We thank You, we believe, we trust, and we receive. In Jesus' name. Amen.

MINISTRY CONFESSION

Father God, we love You with all our hearts, and with all our souls, and with all our minds. This is the first and great commandment. And the second is like unto it, Thou shalt love thy neighbor as thyself. On these two commandments I hang all the law and the prophets as You have instructed me to do.

Thank you, God, for giving us whatever we ask, according to Your Word, because we keep Your commandments, and do those things that are pleasing in Your sight. Thank you, God, for dwelling in us, as we dwell in You, and Your Spirit is dwelling in us. Thank you for being filled with Your Holy Spirit and we have power to work the work You have called chose and commissioned us to. Thank you, God, for allowing Your will to be done.

Father, thank you as we pray in the Holy Ghost You show us how to receive all Your promises, provisions, and promotions, You have released to prosper us. Thank you, Father, for giving us Your plans, which have to be carried out by man, and it's all in our hands. Thank you for helping us to always stand.

We never covet anyone else's ministry. Our ministry is divinely designed and predestined for each of us. Thank you, God, for it's in You that we put our trust. Father, thank you as we speak to mountains and they are removed and casted into the sea. We have no doubt in our hearts and what we say You allow to come to pass. We thank You that we receive the desires of our hearts, and You are never far. As we draw near to You, You draw near to us.

Thank you, Father, for our ministry. It is what You want it to be, as we follow Your will and Holy Ghost leadership. I believe and I receive. In Jesus' name. Amen.

Introduction

I'm so thankful! I'm so amazed! I'm so excited! I'm expecting! I'm encouraged! I'm experiencing! This is another awesome book of revealed secrets from God, which He has blessed me to write, and I know it will bless the body of Christ. I began writing this book, November 19, 2014 and finished on November 7, 2015. God has spoken to me, He's speaking to me now, and shall continue to speak to me, concerning the things that have happened, is happening, and shall continue to happen in our lives. Believers must believe these two key truths:

1) God is NOT a man.
2) God DOES NOT lie.

God is not a man, so he does not lie. He is not human, so he does not change his mind. Has he ever spoken and failed to act? Has he ever promised and not carried it through? (Numbers 23:19 NLT)

We must keep trusting and have the faith that believes God has already done it. Whatever our IT is, it's done. Remember the key is to love God.

Jesus replied, You must love the LORD, your God, with all your heart, all your soul, and all your mind. (Matthew 22:37 NLT)

This book came about from the words of a prophet. God says believe His prophets so shall we prosper.

And they rose early in the morning, and went forth into the wilderness of Tekoa: and as they went forth, Jehoshaphat stood and said, Hear me, O Judah, and ye inhabitants of Jerusalem; Believe in the Lord, your God, so shall ye be established; believe his prophets, so shall ye prosper. (2 Chronicles 20:20 KJV)

When Apostle Dr. Leroy Thompson spoke these words, "that we should pray and ask God to show us how to walk in our prosperity: and then we should pray in the Holy Ghost at least 15 minutes or more every day, hear, listen, and do what He says do, and God will give us wisdom on how to get all He has already given us; because of the finished work of Christ Jesus."

I choose to say it like this, "The victory is won because of God's Son." Praise God!

I obeyed the prophet, and started doing what he said. I thank God for His prophets, and using Apostle Dr. Leroy Thompson to speak those words to me. I thank God for choosing me, and I'm a willing vessel wanting to be used by Him. These words I speak are from God, by way of His Holy Spirit, spoken through me. Jesus says it this way,

"Believest thou not that I am in the Father, and the Father in me? The words that I speak unto you I speak not of myself: but the Father that dwelleth in me, he doeth the works." (John 14:10 KJV)

Praise God! Hear, listen, and do. Get the wisdom on how God wants to get His blessings to you. God gives you a plan, however it has to be carried out by man, and He wants the prosperity in your hands. Thank you, God! Blessings always!

Divine Disclosures of Best Kept Secrets

November 19, 2014@11:11 AM

Money is chasing me down. Angels are loaded down with my money. Money has found me. I have an overflow, outpouring, and overtaking of money. I have the favor of God. I have rivers of money. I have been made a God made miracle millionaire. Businesses have found me to show me favor, and give me money. Customers are coming from everywhere, they are attracted to my products, and they buy in abundance. I have businesses across this world, and several employees. My money has prosperity, it continues to grow, and no man can stop my prosperity, because it's divinely given by God.

I sow in abundance as I receive bountifully. The kingdom has plenty of money, because of my enormous seeds. Holy Spirit gives me the wisdom of my sowing always. I never sow in bad soil. I'm never manipulated out of my money. I have wisdom, knowledge, and understand of my prosperity, and this is why my prosperity is continually coming to me. My children are blessed in abundance, my family, friends, and kingdom are the better because of my prosperity.

November 19@11:15 AM

The race isn't given to the swift or the strong, but to those that endure to the end. You have endurance money; your prosperity is everlasting. Your money has come to you in bundles. Every time one bundle is opened another bundle comes in. The bundles never stop opening, and they never stop coming in.

You have launched out into the deep, and you are receiving boatloads of money. Reel it in. Money has bombarded your bank account. Money that you didn't know was coming or how it came, it's just deposited. Supernatural deposits are released because of the favor, from the favor-givers, now.

You are a favor giver, it's all designed for you to win, and My kingdom to increase, says the almighty God. Money always finds you. Money is attracted to you. You are a money magnet. Money is no problem. You are a MONEY PROBLEM SOLVER. People will come to you for wisdom on how to make money, keep money, and distribute money to the kingdom first, and then their houses; and the businesses you have.

You have My wisdom wealth and Word on every situation that's presented to you. My Word never returns void, it accomplishes what I tell it to do, and prospers where I sent it. My Word always overrides any other word, even your word. Stay tuned to my channel, listen to my voice, and no other voice, obey me, and serve me only, and you shall always prosper, be in health, even your soul shall prosper.

Always be willing to follow me even when it looks ridiculous to you, just hear, listen, and do, everything as unto Me, your almighty most high God. I have sent the reign, its reigning resources, revenue, and riches. Wealth and riches belong to you. It's placed in your house, no one can stop or take it away, and wealth is here to stay. My wealth comes to you every day.

You will never go another day without money coming your way. Angels are programmed to take your money right to you. Angels are always in route to your house, loaded down with your money, MONEY HAS COME TO YOU NOW!!!

November 20@12:35 PM

Because you have done the ridiculous, you have received the miraculous. You are not ashamed of Me; I'm not ashamed of you. You are blessed beyond measure, and people will see I have done this work in you. They now know what blessings look like.

They have also seen what curses look like. Being broke is a curse, not having enough is a curse, and lack is a curse. Having more than enough, overflowing, overloaded, and loaded down with my blessings is what I have preserved, promised, and promoted you for.

Keep pushing, pressing, and preparing for the prosperity, it's never ending because I have allowed it to come; not by your might, but by My spirit, says your all mighty, miraculous, always causing you to receive My miracles, God. I'm the one and only Lord of the harvest, my harvest is plentiful.

Keep sowing because I have made you a reaper, even in places you haven't sown. You are the owner, originator, and overseer of the harvest; therefore no one, and nothing can ever take from you, what I have allow to come to past. Your prosperity will always last. Hear, listen, and do everything as unto Me.

Everything I give to you comes quickly, suddenly, right now. It's yours for the asking, it's all in my will, and you have asked of Me receive now, It's My pleasure!!!

November 26@9:42 AM

The 10 IN's of Wealth:
1) Insight
2) Inquire
3) Initiate
4) Investigate
5) Inspire
6) Instructions
7) Invite
8) In vision
9 Income
10) Increase

I have given you these Ten IN's of Wealth; you must follow them my way first, according to Matthew 6:33. When you seek My kingdom first, and My righteousness, then I will add all things unto you. This is the only way to receive, and retain, My promises, and prosperity, that I have already preserved, for you, and because you have asked according to My will. I heard you, and shall give you the desires of your heart, as long as you allow your desires to line up with what I positioned you to receive. Never cease to follow My plan I have given you, make that your plan for yourself, and others who I will send to you, to teach them my ways.

These 10 INs of Wealth are My wisdom, word, and way, that I chose for you, and the body of your Lord, and Savior Jesus Christ, so take them, eat them, and drink, because I give you this for my Son's sake. Always remember the cross experience. Jesus death, burial, and resurrection. The price was paid for you to receive, reap, and render service, back to Me. It's all for my kingdom sake. My kingdom is at hand, My kingdom shall always stand, and as always I chose to use man.

December 3@12:39 PM

You can never afford to think broke again. I have made you to win. Angels are ascending and descending; they are going to heaven bringing your money back to you on earth. They are loaded down with your money. You have happy money, money that has no sorrow. Don't listen to broke mined people ever again. They will cause you not to win.

I have made you rich and wealthy; and wealth and riches are in your house now. You have the money cometh anointing on you, no one can take it from you; only you can give it away. Stay in my righteousness. Live right all the time.

You must call, confess, command, money to come, and expect it to come. Never doubt, because it allows you to lose out. You are a money magnet. Money as found you. Money is attracted to you, and money is attached to you.

You have believed My prophets, so are you prospering, and not just seven years of straight blessings, however, fourteen years of continual blessings, coming to you NOW! You don't need to know how right now, just know it's coming, and look for it. Doors of wealth are open, and money has entered into your house, and overtaking you, your children, and grandchildren.

You will never be broke another day in your life. Never worry about what's going out your hand, always know what's coming in, don't see money as leaving, however, always see money increasing. That's the money I have given you. That's the key to your continual wealth.

Wealthy people always look for ways to get more money, not what they will lose. You have received your miracle millions for My kingdom sake. You have received your money that's added unto you because you seek My kingdom first and foremost. Never stop sowing, as money continues to harvest. The crops have come up.

There can never be a continual flowing, without continual sowing. The seeds are what make the harvest come up. Make sure it's in the right soil. Never sow in the wrong soil. You will block and stop your harvest. It doesn't matter what you think or who you feel should have or you should give to, I have given you these millions, and I chose who you should give to or bless.

Every seed sown must be from the prompting of My Holy Spirit. You have wisdom from Me, your almighty God, to continue to get wealth. The authority is yours. I have given you the knowledge and understand along with it. Know and always have understanding what to do. Know I will always use you.

There are no limits to my ladder, and levels, leap as high as I continual to take you. I need you and you need Me, let's work together in this harvest field, because the white fields, I have opened, and already harvested for you. Receive all my promises, prosperity, promotions and I'm pleased to give it all to you.

December 7@7:44 AM

You have BIG, GIGANTIC, ENORMOUS money. Step into your season of increase. This is your time of breakthrough favor in every area of your life. I'm blessing you with money you haven't seen or ever had before. Men shall give unto your bosom. Your broke days are over never to return again.

You have creative ideas and witty inventions, and they are coming out of you now. You have the gift of sightseeing. You create ideas in your spiritual imagination and the outcome is seen in the natural. People will pay for the ideas you create.

You have wisdom to get wealth. Your thoughts are the thoughts that I give you. Always keep your mind clear to hear me, your almighty all powerful God. Keep your ears tentative to my voice and my instructions.

You are the first to go and see places no one in your generation as ever seen or been before. Your daughter is the next generation. Her graduating, is the beginning of this spiritual realm, this high ranking; is a place where eyes have not seen nor ears heard, a place for you because you love, Me and I love you. There is nothing that I won't ever do for you, as long as you continue to walk in my righteousness, and seeking my kingdom first.

Everything you imagine and couldn't have imagined to do, and it's according to my will, and My promises, provision, promotions, and I shall always bring it to pass. People shall give unto your bosom, as I command them to do. Everything always works for your good. Keep working My principles as I have reserved all these weeks of harvest which never stop coming to you. It's my pleasure to prosper you. Enjoy!

December 8@8:21 AM

There is more money coming in than going out if your hands. The harvest is plenteous but the laborers are few. All this harvest is for you. I am no respecter of persons what I have done for Apostle Dr. Leroy Thompson, I have done the same in principle for you.

You must work My principles every day, obey, and serve Me, regardless of what comes your way. I have made a way even when you couldn't see your way. It's your day of endless revelations and they are here to stay. You are anointed, and have power to get my wealth.

Always listen to the sound that your Lord, and savior Jesus Christ sends you, and you will always win. Know that's it's My wealth that you are walking in. It's My favor, and not your labor. My yolk is easy, and burdens are light. When you walk in my wealth you must live right.

Never step away from what I gave you today. If you do this wealth, wisdom, and Word will go away. Receive of me, your almighty God, everyday, because wealth is here to stay. Enjoy!

Things you have when walking in God.

1) Supernatural of Wealth
2) Supply of Wind
3) Servant is Willing
4) Saturated in the Word
5) Sound in Wisdom
6) Strong in Worship
7) Source is Wonderful

December 9@11:35 AM

You have pulled the level and released money. Truckloads of money are coming to you today. I'm dumping it off at your house NOW! Expect exceedingly, abundantly, above all that you could have asked me for. Open the door. I have given money entrance permission into your house; let it in. Receive your shipment today.

When you do the ridiculous you receive the miraculous. Go knock down the door with your fist, open it up, and touch down the door NOW! Keep your eyes focused on me. See what I see, and not what you see. Say what I say and what I have said.

My sight, and sound, overrules your sight, and sound. There's always a rhythm in the beat. The beat has to come from you, and the rhythm is from Me. You must receive the rhythm from Me. You receive it from the spiritual realm, and mix it with your natural. Together it's supernatural. You live in the supernatural.

Your ears must stay tentative, turned, and tuned, into My channel. This is the way you live. You asked for it you got it. Never look back, regardless of what's trying to jump on your back.

Weapons will form, but they shall not prosper. Don't be afraid of the weapons, because you are equipped for war. I have equipped My servants. You are the called out ones from me. Always hear, listen, and do, everything unto me, your almighty all-powerful God. I put the fight in you. Always fight the good fight of faith.

The horn is blowing on the train, it's an indication you are on the right track, and moving in the right direction, it's also a warning for people to move out of your way. The enemy has no choice but to move. He will move, or else be run over, and destroyed. This is My job, the destroying; your job is to keep blowing the horn — speaking My Word continually.

Stay on track, moving in My direction, never looking back, speaking to the enemy warning them to get out the way. I shall continue to move them, and manifest the destinations, and allow you to make it to them all. Money is mighty, more than enough, mounted, and manifested in your hands NOW! Enjoy!

December 10@8:24 AM

I have opened the sea for you walk through. Every place that the soles of your feet thread upon, I have given to you. This earth is mine, and the fullness thereof, and they that dwell therein, because its mine; such as I have I give to you. I am your Sheppard, you are my sheep; you follow after me, and no one else.

When you seek, you shall always find, every time you knock the door shall be open to you. Ask of me, and I give you the desires of your heart, when you do your part. I am with you even before you start. I ordained you before you entered into your mother's womb. I chose, commanded, and commissioned, you to go, and you never shall go empty, and this why in the beginning I gave you dominion.

I said be fruitful, multiply, subdue, and replenish. Every time you give out, more comes in. Sowing, and reaping until the end. You always win. You have wealth and riches in your house. Use what you got.

I will cause people to find you, and purchase from you at retail value. What you have is worth the price because my hand is in it. I allow you to create designs straight from My Holy Spirit. People don't decide your prosperity that I give to you, your almighty, all-powerful God.

What one isn't willing to pay, others customers are always on the way. Never allow your discounts to deplete you. Stand firm; never be afraid of your prices. You and your customers are a mix. You have what they want, precious, and priceless products; and they have what you want plenty money, moving, and manifesting, to you.

Never be afraid of the price; it's no problem because you are precious in my sight and so are the products I allow you to create. Enjoy!

December 11@10:01 AM

1) Seed
2) Sower
3) Servant
4) Source
5) Supernatural
6) Surplus
7) Supply

I have given you these seven things to multiply. You are the apple in My eye, and it's good for the eating. You have been raised up for such a time as this. The apple was never bad, the bad was the disobedience of Eve that ate it. My fruit is always good, and I have chosen, charged, and commissioned, you to bare much fruit. Stay in obedience to My will, which is My Word, and receive My wealth continually.

Never be disturbed, disappointed, or distracted, by the enemy, he only has a bark, and not a bite; as the weapons are formed, they shall never prosper. What you allow me to do for you, shall always bring fruit in your season, and prosper you.

Again I say to you, this is your season of breakthrough favor in your life. Money has come to you NOW, and shall never stop coming. You have an overflow, overtaken, outpouring, of money NOW; it shall always be more than enough, and never not enough.

Again money is here to stay, and always on the way. Remember to never stop calling money, as it never stop obeying you, and coming to you. I am showing, and my revelations are for your knowing. I am your almighty all-powerful God. Make sure My Word never departs for your heart. Keep them coming out your mouth daily, speaking life, and not death, blessings, and not curses. Watch me send men to give to you, when you do what I say to do. Enjoy!

December 11@10:12 AM

You have a new life in Me, you are dead to sin alive in Me. Old things are passed away, behold all things are new. No one can take you where I'm taking you. Your old life can't exist anymore; you had to let it go to receive this new life in Me. I am doing a new thing in you don't worry or be afraid, just hear, listen, and do, everything as unto Me.

Watch me as I have already prepared, preserved, and promise, people for the vision. You shall live like the queen you are, People will come from near, and far, to serve Me, and serve you, My kingdom is at hand, your life has expanded; it's all in your hands. Use your gift as I have given you, and commanded you to.

Money isn't a problem. I have plenty, and it's yours for the asking. Wealth, and riches, is yours now. Today is your day of breakthrough favor. People have heard from me, and the wealth has come. One moment of favor is far worth a lifetime of labour. The harvest has come because it's my will being done. Enjoy, it's my pleasure, and it's popping time, the explosion has begun, and money has exploded into your hands.

December 14@12:46 PM

God says he's brought us through our situations, circumstances, and into our promises, provisions, promotions, and prosperity. God already knows what he gone do, shame on you if you go back through. Always be thankful, and have ears to hear what He has to say.

You are blessed of God, and you are on your way, partially because of what you have done today. Enjoy the fruits of your labor, because God has brought you out of labor into His favor. Never go back to where you have been, if you do, you will never win. I have allowed you to triumph in every situation that you were in.

These words that I speak aren't just for your marriage, but also for your ministry, and for miracles, that's moving mightily, and motivated, to manifest into your hands. Enjoy all these kingdom blessings because you have heard what I had to say, and you must continue to do it all My way.

December 17@8:02 AM

Spiritual Takeover has hit your life. It overrides, and cancels any thoughts, things, temptation, and trumps over the flesh today. You are spiritual minded, you have life, and peace, you always walk in the spirit not the flesh, you are lead by the spirit, it has taken over the flesh. Flesh has no good things, My spirit has everything. I have allowed you to live out your BIG DREAMS, because you have dared to dream.

Creative ideas and witty inventions are coming out of you NOW!!! They are coming in threes. They are meeting the needs of my kingdom, because My kingdom is at hand. You have met the demand. Spiritual takeover is in your hand. Your flesh can't stand, because your spirit is the man.

You abide in the override. Spirit break out, breaking the walls down. The walls are down, the doors are open, the wealth, and riches, are in, never to leave again, they have no end. You have ever increasing income, impartation, instructions, and you continue in My Word, your almighty, all-powerful, God.

I shall continue to give you My Word, wisdom, and wealth, and teach you my way, which is the only way, to live life, and life more abundantly. Always pay attention to the sound, rhythm, and beat. I have released the sound, the rhythm, and beat, it comes from you.

Again stay close to the sound, hear, listen, and do, I can't do your part for you. You have your job, I got mine, and it's all a matter of time. Spiritual Takeover is in charge, everything else has to depart, and it's destroyed. I have done this. The lane is opened, you are on the straight and narrow path, and everyone can't fit into your lane.

You have my entrance permission; enter into My large place of wealth, where no one can take, and this you didn't make. It's all for My name's sake. Enjoy!!!

December 17@6:07 PM
1) Ships are Docked
2) Supernaturally And Delivered
3) Sufficient and Dominion
4) Servants are Destined
5) Spiritually and Discerned
6) Savior and Director

Keep confessing money is coming, because of the promise. All these things I speak to you today, is the way your wealth shall continue to come. Remember to sound the alarm. My wealth won't cause you any harm. I have filled your barns.

Overflow, overflow, overflow, I give you plenty more. Endless blessings, spiritual takeover, you can't lose, you are My example, encourager, and you have evidence of My large wealthy place; all because you didn't get out of the race. This wasn't given to the swift, nor the strong, but to you who endured until the end. Because you made it to the end, I have allowed things to come to an end for you.

Lack has ended, just enough has ended, abundance, always abounding, has begun for you. You have won the race, I allowed you to run. The finish is on. You must never stop. Continue on. The harvest has come. There's no ending to your sowing, showing, and growing, enjoy!

December 19@8:55 AM
I'm in charge of money, its goes where I tell it to go, and does what I say do. Money is my slave. Just like the waves are subject to the wind, money has been blown in like a mighty rushing wind. I have authority over money. I'm Lord over my money. I protect my money. Money has been called to my house. Money has found me. I have let money in.

I'm walking in the newness in life, this life of more than enough, this life of riches in Christ Jesus. I stay on the path of righteousness, the straight and narrow path. I walk in the fullness of almighty, all-powerful God. I'm a MONEY CARRIER. Money is attracted to me, attached to me, and I have received abundance of money NOW. The kingdom is rich because of the money I have received.

I meet the needs of the kingdom because of the money that's been given me. I have a right to my money. I have power to get my wealth. I have no more empty hands. Money is always in high demand. Receive these revelations from me NOW!!!

My speech determines my reach. I have what I say. Money is here to stay. My broke days are over. I have more than enough for the kingdom of God and for my house. Wealth and riches are in my house. I have divine breakthroughs in every area of my life. God has brought me out. No more debt. Supernatural increase is in my house. I'm a God-made miracle millionaire!!! I receive and enjoy!!!

December 19@9:00 AM

Because you have sowed in the days of famine your brooks shall never run dry. Same year blessings are on you, as Isaac did so have you. All these blessings shall on you, and continue to overtake you in your going in, and your coming out, praise me with a loud shout. I have brought you out.

What I have done for one in principle I have caused to come to you. Continue in My Word, speak My language, stay together on one accord, I will give you things that at one time you couldn't afford. Receive what you want, your heart desires, never worry about what you can't afford. I give you more than enough, because you are on board.

This ship docks in places you have never seen before. Countries welcome you. This world, I have given you. Hear, listen, and do everything I say to do. It's all designed just for you.

Flowers, and Lilies grow with nurturing; you grow with the intake, increase, impartation, of My Word, in season, and out of season. You prosper for this very reason. You have the finer things in life, and it is to see what it's all about, and live abundant life without any doubt. I have worked it all out enjoy!

December 28@11:55 AM

The seed of the righteous is blessed. You have HEAVY SEEDS. Your seeds are packed, and pressed down, you have so much seeds to sow, and so much seeds you know. I have revealed to you where to sow. Go where I say go. The seeds are weighted down with HEAVY HARVEST. They both work together in the fields of increase.

Your fields are overflowing, and outpouring, with HEAVY SEEDS AND HEAVY HARVEST. The crops have come up. The rain is here. You are ruling, resting, rendering, and receiving, all my promises, promotions, and prosperity. If it wasn't so, I would not have told you.

Again white fields are already harvested, you are my peculiar people, chosen generation, royal priesthood, and this is the generation of the upright. The seed of the righteous are blessed, your children are blessed, and their children are blessed, wealth, and riches, are in your house.

Supernatural wealth is yours for the asking, it's according to my will, and I have caused you to prosper, and I'm pleased to prosper you. I am your all mighty, all powerful God. Consistency is My will. Continue to pray. Continue in My Word that's consistency. I honor your consistency. It will continue to carry you, and because you to continue in My wealth that I have given you power to get. Enjoy!!!

December 24@8:18 AM

Quick Money: On the plane you look outside and see the clouds then close your eyes, and still see the clouds in your mind, that's how quick I'm going to give you your wealth. Again don't be concerned with what you see right now, it's only temporary. My money comes in a hurry.

Just keep obeying My will, following My instructions, hearing My voice, spoken through My prophets, so shall you continue to prosper. Keep your standards high; you will never just get by. I'm giving you dreams of people with wealth. It's all for the example of where you have been elevated to receive of Me your all mighty, all powerful, God.

Your wealth is here; stay focused. Don't fear, things you see right now, they are not as they appear. Enjoy!!!

December 31@9:40 AM

God allowed us to fly. God allowed us to multiply, from caterpillar to butterfly. You have your wings NOW SOAR! I have said to you before, it's Soaring Time. I have blessed you NOW more than ever before. You have your wings; watch me do new things.

I have given you this platform, and positioned you for all My promises, provisions, and promotions. Where I am there you shall be also. What I say you shall say also. What I do you shall do also. Greater works you shall do because you are My beloved child, you have accepted My beloved Son, and you worship Me with all your heart, mind, body, and soul.

You worship Me in spirit, and in truth, because My will for you is to worship Me in spirit and in truth, as you have come forth to do. Stay hidden, the devil can only seek after you, don't allow yourself to be revealed to him. He can only see when you reveal yourself to him. You are hidden in Me under My wings, never peek out to see where, or what he's doing, don't pay attention to what the enemy does.

Worship gets My attention, it's comes from My heart to yours, as you worship Me expect all open doors; even doors that was shut. Doors that have been shut shall never be opened again. Doors that Satan shut are opened again. It's all designed for you to win.

You are the apple of My eye. Why? Because you are fruitful, and I have allowed you to multiply. Sometime I speak to you in parables, you hear me in the spirit, and walk it out in the natural. Your spirit man shall always be feeding, focusing, and found hearing, listening, and doing my will, your all mighty, all powerful God.

Keep soaring, sowing, and expecting the supernatural surplus and supply that comes from your source, sustainer, and all-sufficient God. Enjoy!!!

December 31@12:24 PM

It's your time, and season of breakthrough favor. You have my wealth and riches in your house. My angels are loaded down, and continue to bring bundles, and bundles, of money to you. Money never stops flowing as I never stop showing, your almighty, all-powerful God.

I have allowed people to see where you are going; however they are not going with you. They only can only see where I'm taking you. The people I send will tell you they are sent by me, through dreams, visions, or thoughts, that I have given them about you. I've put you on people mind to help in the prosperity process to prosper My kingdom and your house.

I've released material things that you didn't ask me for. Your job is to be fruitful, multiply, replenish, subdue, and have dominion always. I'm pleased to prosper you. You are my beloved children, heirs, and joint heirs, with My Son, your savior, Jesus Christ. Because you are in Christ Jesus, made in My image you shall always receive, and have dominion.

Stick with the rhythm, and beat, always hearing from me. Never go a day without hearing, listening, and doing, as I say, wealth and riches shall always stay, and it's on the way coming to you today. Continue to be consistent in sowing seeds, as I shall continue to allow the harvest to come, and never run out. Your job is seed sowing, and My job is knowing and releasing the harvest. You don't have to know how, just expect to receive. Just remember these words I have given you.

1) Anointed
2) Actions
3) Activate
4) Access
5) Abundant
6) Always abounding
7) Anchored

Keep My commands continue to follow My instructions, and shall I make it all happen for you, enjoy!!!

January 9, 2015@6:23 AM

You have reached your peak, the highest level of anointing. Always sow your supernatural, divinely directed, peak seeds, and you shall always receive the highest levels of supernatural, divinely directed harvest, straight from Me, your almighty, all-powerful, all sufficient God.

Don't be afraid to make the connection, don't worry about the cost, the connection is far greater than the cost of the connection. Where you going you can't afford not to connect. The soil is so fertile right now, again, the crops have come up, never let money stop you from doing what I say do.

Again, don't look at what you got; look at what's coming in. God knows both ends. Harvest time is here. Seven years of blessings and plenty are here, and the cycle keeps repeating, enjoy!!!

January 13@3:02 PM

My supernatural seven years of plenty is here. I'm anointed to access, and activate, the abundance. I receive my increase NOW! My overflowing, overtaking, and outpouring of blessings are overshadowing everything that the enemy tried to stop, and stagnate me with. I'm lost in the presence of God. Holy Spirit has taken me to the strength of the King.

I'm up on the inside of Jesus, and God. I'm living on the inside of God, and I'm in Christ Jesus. Holy Spirit is my helper. The blood has blocked every hindrance spirit. I'm living in the most high and holy faith.

My finances and favor has finally found me. I will never go back to my broke days, and not enough days. I have more than enough. I'm wealthy and rich and it's a continual flow, and it's flooding, and flourishing in my finances. I have called, commanded, and commissioned, money cometh to me now, and it's here supernaturally, straight from the sustainer, and source, my almighty, all-powerful, all sufficient God. The one and only, that I say W.O.E. to I'm Willing Obedient and Eating the good of the land. The one who is my B.O.S.S., as I Be an

Obedient, Servant, and Spend, my days in prosperity, and my years in pleasure.

I thank my God for all He has preserved, promoted, and promised me, and I receive my manifested, release NOW! I'm enjoying!!!

January 21@5:27 PM

You are in a land where there is no scarcity, a land of no lack, a land of brooks of waters, of fountains and depths, that spring out of valley, and hills, a land that flows with milk and honey, a land of plenty money, a land where the blessings keep coming, a land of laughter, and enjoyment, this land is your land, and I have placed it all in your hands. You have unlimited reach it's all at your feet. Because you placed it at my feet.

The Altar, Atmosphere, Accesses the Anointing. Receive of Me Abundance, Always abounding, and ever-increasing, seven years, of seven fold, manifold blessings, from Me. Your Almighty, All-powerful, all-sufficient God. The earth is mine, and the fullness there off, and I have given it to you that dwell there in.

Continue praying, and praising Me, which I commanded you to do. You have received all my promises that I have released to you. Now and forever. I have commanded you to do a new thing; you are in the strength of the King, and receiving everything.

You are a new creation; you have control over this nation. Old things are passed away; behold all is new. You are in a new zone. I never leave you alone. I'm always with you even until the end of this world.

Forget about the past. Keep pushing, pressing, till you get to the Mark of the prize of the higher calling in Christ Jesus. As Jesus made a Mark and you are in Christ Jesus, so shall you, when you do as I say to do.

You are marked with increase, impartation, and information. I give increase as Holy Spirit imparts information directly divinely from me. Stay humble never prideful. Queens off the Castle have been birthed from you.

Never be afraid, or alarmed. People will see what I have done. Money will never be a problem. Follow My plan, and process, promotions, and prosperity shall continue to come. You are my God made miracle millionaire. Queens of the Castle is the fruit I've allowed you to birth, and bare. It shall multiply and remain as seed time and harvest time never ceased. The delivery has begun and babies are being born. Receive Now!!!

I have brought you out to help bring them out. Your big dreams are now reality because you sought Me and My kingdom first, now everything else is added unto you. This is what I'm pleased to do. Enjoy!!!

January 27@3:45 PM

I have anointed you to prosper. I shall do things for you that I have never done before. You shall do things for me you have never done before. I have opened the doors. Enter into My place of peace, pleasures, promises, promotions, and prosperity, all from me, your almighty, all-powerful God. You shall never depart, I shall never depart, and you are always in my heart, as I am yours.

I have opened many doors. You have my seven fold manifold blessings, the white fields are already harvested, its harvest time, the crops have come in. They are picked, pruned, and preserved, especially for you; now you know what to do. I have brought you out, now give me a shout, and continue to praise me.

I have released the favor, now people will use the power, ability, and influence, to help you, as they do as I say do. You are a favor giver as you pray, praise, operate in the prophetic, and preach My Word. In season and out of season.

I have chosen, called, commissioned, and charged you. You have been through the valley of the shadow of death and have come out without any evidence that you went through. The scars are removed because of the way you went through.

I ordained you a prophet before you entered into your mother's womb. Make room make room there is no more doom. You are delivered, dominating, and deserving of my seven fold, manifold blessings. Live, laugh, and love this life I have given you.

I've anointed you to have a great marriage, ministry, and overflow, outpouring, and overtaken of money. You will teach people the world says are unteachable, and reach those who are unreachable. You have My unusual favor and grace on you. Always do as I say do regardless of what comes to you, because of your life changing experiences.

Marriages, ministries, and monies will change in their favor. People you lay hands on shall be healed immediately, everything and everyone you touch prospers. Supernatural breakthroughs are manifested and released quickly, sudden NOW!

Testimonies shall come forth like never seen or heard of before; curses are broken as the word is spoken. You have a speaking spirit. Supernatural souls are coming forth NOW!!! Supernatural increase NOW!!! Enjoy!!!

January 29@9:24 AM

I'm in charge and control over everything in my life. I give people help that want it. God has shielded and protection me from all danger. He's given me His Holy Spirit to help me and hide me that I'm safe from all troubles.

The enemy can't get close to me even when he comes after me, and chases me. He can't see me and he can't touch me, because I'm hidden under the shadow of Gods wings, in His secret pavilion. The enemy will try to grab me, however God clothe and surrounds me in His place of safety and security.

Holy Spirit shows me the doors that are open unto me and I know when and where to enter in. I run into the doors God has allowed to open, and into God's place of provision, promises, and promotions. I help those that want to be helped and show them what's required to live this life of peace, protection, and prosperity.

Holy Spirit helps me to see where God wants me to go, as I quickly receive everything I want from God, as I show others who want to move into this new place of opportunity, outpouring, overflowing and overtaking of God's seven fold, manifold blessings, that only comes from Him. Praise God from whom all blessings flow!

Through Holy Spirit I shall continue to know and grow. Hallelujah!!!

January 31@1:44 AM

I have blessed you indeed. I have enlarged your territory. My hand is with thee; no evil shall hurt you, or come near your dwelling place as you are indwelling in me. Souls are saved; supernaturally they are coming from the north, south, east, and west. No more addictions, deliverance is here, healing is here, to all who will receive and believe in Me, your almighty, all-powerful, all-sufficient God, that never will depart, because His heart in your heart. No more stress, struggle, and strain you are in my vain.

As I told your before all sufferings are out the door you are living under an open heaven the heavens are open many doors are open to those that live righteous, live by My standards, statues, and My and spirit. The king is here have no fear.

The reign is here, receive your harvest, the crops have come up, because of your seeds you have met the needs of the kingdom first now everything is added unto you continue to do as I say do and everything will always work for you. Your service will never be ordinary but extraordinary. Never make excuses because you are operating in the supernatural and you shall always receive in the supernatural. Supernatural healing, deliverance, and increase shall always be yours and to those who want to follow your ministry and the wisdom that I speak through you.

Money shall never be a problem. Marriages shall always be protected, your ministry shall prosper, and all my promises are released to you. You are living in the seven years of plenty there will never be a drought; even in the famine years you shall always be satisfied.

Stay disciplined, determined, destined to do everything from your heart. Keep your heart right with me and this allows you to keep it right with people. I gave you favor and no hard labor. Continue to work for me and I shall continue to do it all for you. It's my pleasure! Enjoy!!!

February 3@2:18 PM

Doing a new thing in 2015: I'm Praying in the spirit everyday and more than ever before, worshiping and praising God with all my heart making sure He never departs. I'm focused on marriage, ministry, and money. I'm receiving what God has in store, which is more than ever before.

My storehouses, which are my savings, are full with plenty. I have a P&L Statement. The world calls it Profit & Loss...I call it Prosperity and no Lack. I'm willing and obedient and eating the good of the land. I'm obeying and serving God and spending my days in prosperity and my years in pleasure.

I'm enjoying the finer things in life, I know what the not so finer things are I'm experiencing and living in the best that God has for me. My life is full of joy, peace, love, and laughter. Thank God for allowing me to Do a New Thing. I love this life I'm living more abundantly!!! Praise God!!!

February 5@3:21 PM

There's no hindrance spirit that can stop your harvest. You have done the sowing now your money is flowing, flooding, flourishing, and what you made happen for Me and My kingdom I shall always make happen for you, hear, listen, and do it all unto Me, your almighty all powerful God creator of all. Continue to follow Me you will never fall.

I've given you visions as well as dreams you shall know what they mean. Keep your hearts clean. What I have created in you no one can tell you it's not from me. Holy Spirit shall always be your guide and I'm always on your side.

As I've said before you have more and more I've opened doors no man can shut, so never give up. Keep seeking and knocking you have asked Me once no need to ask again, you are a winner, as long as you continue in My Word, worship and praise me.

Obedience is better than sacrifice; never give up your righteousness for what looks right to you do as I say do. If you didn't hear from me through Holy Spirit it didn't come from me. What looks like a blessing to you is a curse from the enemy doing what he knows to do. Check your space and the people that come in it. Especially the ones that recently came in.

Don't get emotional; it's not from me. The past is the past. If you allow them to enter in you will not win.

You are doing a new thing in now; old things and people are passed away from you life in the past and future. Don't let your childhood take you back to thinking it's all good. Hear me; I'm the one that brought you out.

Always speaking to your spouse, don't allow the enemy in your house. Just because people say they have changed doesn't mean it's in my name. Hear, listen, and do.

I've made the way for you straight and narrow is the gate I do everything for my name sake, my one and only Son, Jesus Christ, as you are in Christ Jesus always be led by Holy Spirit which is in you. Enjoy!!!

February 9@9:39 AM

It's already done we have won … victory, victory, victory! It's all because of My Son. You have tapped into the supernatural things from Me, your all mighty all-powerful God. I have always been with you from the start.

The outpouring is here in your atmosphere. It's on you. You know what to do, because I shall continue to show you. You are My heart I'm in your heart. We work together in the harvest field that's white and has already been harvested for you.

As I was with Moses so am I with you. Stretch out your rod, and I shall open the Red Sea and you shall and have received from Me.

The rivers are flowing and I'm showing. I'm showing off in you because you have allowed Me to. Continue to watch me do a work in you. People shall marvel at what I have done for you. They will know who I AM through what I have done and continue to do for you.

Your children are blessed and your children's children are blessed. This is the generation of the upright; because you have gotten it so have they. You are the model, mentor, motivator, minister, and mantel of their manifestation.

The manifestation release is on you. You have believed my prophets so are you prospering NOW! My faith is NOW! So live in the NOW because your NOW is always your next and never ending blessings from me.

Continue to live in the supernatural and spiritual realm, which releases everything into your natural realm. Always in that order. You will never fall or fail to be fruitful and financially flourishing and flowing in my kingdom wealth and wealth and riches shall stay in your house and never add sorrow. Enjoy!!!

February 11@7:31 PM

I never settle for less because God has given me His very best. I'm blessed much more than the rest. I shall continue to past every test. God has already made a way of escape.

I triumph in every situation. The enemy never destroys me because God has already defeated him. The hand of The Lord is upon me my marriage ministry and money. I have the water of the Word. I have an excellent spirit and extra favor.

When I pray in tongues I have a direct hotline to God. Nothing is too hard for me to do because I'm willing and obedient I'm eating the good of the land — a land of brooks and hills where the water continues to flow and flood in finances... a land of faithfulness and fruitfulness which shall always remain when I stay in a God's vain.

The blood of Jesus has brought me out. I give God this great shout. I receive from God because His heart is full, and I receive God's love and I have love for myself and others.

I walk in agreement with others like me. The same spirit as Christ Jesus. I have togetherness, teamwork, and a winning spirit. I know that no matter what I win, regardless of the situation in front of me or what

I'm facing, I must go for the goal because I can make it to the end because Gods heart is full and faithful to me.

The victory has already been won; it's done. The game was over before it was begun, because I put it in God's hands and He released it into mine.

The doors are opened unto me. I remember to always do what he says do. I will win if I don't quit. I never give up on God because he will never give up on me.

The lane is opened and I choose to follow through on what He has said to do. He made this way for me. I get in line and walk the straight and narrow path, which is His righteousness, and I receive all He has added unto me. Enjoy the victory!

February 14@11:06 AM

Souls shall come when they see what I have done. I've promoted and prospered you for the kingdom sake, as you have acres of land so does your new church property have acres of land. It's all in my plan.

Step out and into your new home that you own by Grand Homes, original Hampton's model. People will see it's all from me. It's not a gimmick. It's what you picked and I gave it to you because you asked of me and it's according to my will.

I have granted you the desires of your heart. You are my child who has asked of me and you shall always receive from me. When you seek you shall always find and when you knock, the doors are always opened unto you.

Receive! Receive! Receive from me your father, your Almighty God my Son, Jesus Christ and my Holy Spirit. They all come from me as I make them all available to you. Never let them go. This is how you shall always know; hear what I'm saying, listen and know what when and how to do everything exactly as I say do.

I have already made a way for you. Don't hesitant to move because of what you believe I'm saying and I'm not saying. Right now, it's not about what you think it's about believing what I say. Believe and you believe in me as I believe in you.

When I say move, you must know and believe the move is much better than the place you are in now, because if you stay in this place which is comfortable to you you're not doing everything as unto me. You must move out of your comfort zone to receive the home that I gave you to own, by Grand Homes, the original Hampton's model.

People will come to your ministry because I've prepared and placed them there. They will say to you, "I'm sent by God." You will know this is the team, where together everyone achieves more. It's all for my kingdom's sake.

Know the move that you make it's all about my directions and your destinations that I have delivered you for supernatural debt cancelation. You have turned from the wrong and mistakes you have made; now you must know it's My will that has been done. You have won because of my Son. Because you are in Christ Jesus you live from the inside out as you are in him and he's in you, and the outside move is from you.

You are My prophet and you must believe my prophet. I have already shown it all to my prophet. He will speak to you; believe him. Chicago isn't ready for you.

I'm ready for you now. You can't trust them for money right now; they're not listening to me now and they won't hear you right now. When it comes to money, they believe they need their money right now.

You need more than a couple in agreement with their money. The task is far greater than the little money right now. You have entrance permission into the opened doors in the suburban area of Dallas, King's Crossings Estates. Remember, the land and churches I allowed you to see on your travels to your new home, Grand Home Original Hampton's Mode.

The white fields have already been harvested for you. The harvest is plenteous for you I have chosen you as part of the few. The crops have come up and I have named some for you, KMC and Pastor AD and Lady Mary Hatter get the new home that you own NOW!

Step out, walk in, and never be afraid of the move from me. I shall always bring it to pass for you when you do as I say to do. Don't think about how that's not your job; it's mine. You are never to look at behinds, always look forward to the future that I've already prepared preserved and promised you. it's yours for the asking.

Again, receive and forget about what you thought and how you thought it would happen. You asked me and I gave it to you.

Again, do as I say to do and you will never fail. The blessings from me maketh you rich and adds no sorrow.

Again, I've opened the land up for you. Know what to do. I've already made it happen for you. The people I've spoken to are communicating about you. They are listening to and obeying me. They are waiting for you.

Obey! Obey! Obey! It's on the way! Enjoy!!!

February 27@2:39 PM

The release is on. We have won. We are walking in the supernatural things from God. We never stop, even when we get there, because there is a place of manifold, which is many destinations that have been given to us from God. So we must continue in His word wisdom and wealth.

Therefore, we never stop thanking God that when you received His message from us, you didn't think of our words as mere human ideas. You accepted what we said as the very word of God — which, of course, it is. And this word continues to work in you who believe. (1 Thessalonians 2:13 NLT)

Money is showing off in us. The people will see this is the lords doing and it marvelous in our sights. We have kingdom wealth and wealth and riches is in our houses. We live in houses that we didn't build and reap where we haven't sown. Money just keeps on coming to us NOW — even when we don't know how.

We believe God's prophets, so are we prospering. Every word that's been spoken to us from God's prophets we believe and we receive every word from Go. I have extra favor from God.

There's healing from the top of our heads to the souls of our feet. No sickness or disease can destroy me. I choose to live and not die and declare the works of the Lord.

I tell everyone to come see a man that can save anybody and heal and help everybody who's willing and obedient. They will get the good of the land. No more lack or being in want of anything. He is always for you and more than anything in this world that can ever be against you. So says your almighty, all-powerful God.

I'm walking in the supernatural results from God. What He has spoken in times past, in the beginning, is still happening in the now and shall be in the ending. You never have to be in sin. You been delivered and forgiven, so walk therein. Miracles, manifestations and money all are my signs and wonders. Enjoy!

March 5@7:57 AM

Walk with me says the Lord our God. Walk into your seasons, as seasons come every day and throughout the year. That is how my blessings are coming to you, day after day year after year — blessings are here. Your many facets are manifold blessings. Receive, believe and trust me now and forever.

Your seeds have brought you into this harvest and shall keep you receiving in this harvest. Sow seeds like never before. I've opened up the doors; walk in. You have entrance permission, come in and taste and see of the greatness I've granted you.

People will see me for the God that I am. I am that I am, you have placed it in my hands and I've allowed you to stand. Continue to work with me, as I do everything that I placed positioned and promised you because it pleases me to prosper you.

In all you do stay focused in faith and you shall continue in my supernatural finances that I have set in motion to come to you. I've given you the overflow and outpouring of my blessings. It's all because you have followed the divine directions and instructions that only come from me through Holy Spirit to my people and prophets.

Walk on, walk in, and walk through. Continue as I do. Again, I've made it happen for you. Enjoy!!!

March 11@11:14 AM

The enemy is trying to keep people on their backs where he can lay on their chests, press down and choke the life out of them. He can put his hands on their necks while they are on their backs and cover their eyes, then press on their heart and keep them from seeing and being all that God has promised.

Don't allow him to keep you on your back. Get up stand on your feet with your loins guarded. Put on the whole armor of God because you have more power on your feet than on your back. Don't allow him to keep you in lack

When standing you can leap, have hope, healing, and harvest. Remember to continue to stand in all you do. Always know what to do. God has already made it happen for you.

The victory is already won, because of God's Son. Stand strong, strengthen, stable, solid, secure, and succeeding in the supernatural. Enjoy the great life and receive all God's promises!

March 11@11:17 PM

I'm in the Throne Zone. I have come into my own. I have swimming power. Just like fish go from ocean to banks, I have advanced through ranks higher heights and deeper depths nothing can trap in.

I see through visible and invisible things. No weeds and no rocks can stop me even if they are there to block me. I own the Zone. I'm in I never lost because of who I choose.

My sight is keen; I know what I've seen. I'm operating in the supernatural. My natural isn't normal in the spirit realm. I always bring the supernatural in from the spirit realm.

The waves of wealth carry me into every vision, dream and stream of increased inspiration and impartation from God Himself. This Throne Zone I'm in has no top. I have come from the bottom and I'm SOARING: Supernatural Overflowing Always Receiving Increase

Necessary Growth. It's always needed to advance the kingdom of God, which is at hand.

I'm anointed to sing in the spirit. I sing songs of praise and worship in all different languages and interpretations. People will hear songs of worship in their languages and will come to accept Jesus Christ as their Lord and saviour.

Our world is in need and Jesus is the seed. Teach and preach Jesus around the world. There's no top, and you can't be stopped.

March 18@10:02 AM

I'm here; I've never left you or forsaken you. I'm not a man and I can't lie. What I've spoken has already been done for you. You shall always know what to do according to my Holy Spirit. You have asked me and everything you have asked it's done for you.

Take comfort I knowing you are living in the supernatural and what you speak comes to pass. Continue in my word; seek me daily. Follow after me regardless of what you see and hear. If I didn't speak it, don't receive it.

You are on the right track. Don't be afraid of the enemy's attack, just continue to confess and call those things that are not as though they were because they have become.

This light affliction is only for a moment and not for keeps. I've promoted you to take leaps, not stop and drop to the tricks of the enemy. Fiery darts shall pass by your target because you are on course. Stay in the race; it's not given to the swift or strong but to those who endures until the end.

Press toward the goal of the prize of higher calling in Christ Jesus. You are free of debt, sickness, and lack. Supernatural healing, a health harvest and wholeness are yours for the asking. I give you everything you ask because it according to my will and word for your life.

Money shall continue to keep coming to you, regardless of what satan tries to do. Trust that like Jesus is so are you. I've given all these promises to you.

You will always know what to do. You will always hear listen and do what I've commanded you to do. I'm your almighty, all-powerful most high God. Enjoy!!!

March 23@6:05 PM

Stay focus in all you do. I shall bring it to pass. What I do for you will always last. Never get weary in doing well. You shall reap if you faint not. It's your time; it's reaping time. You are mine and it's harvest time. Your due season is here; prepare the atmosphere.

You are anointed to prosper. Get ready to receive all my promises and promotions. What I've promised is here. Receive in the right atmosphere.

You have chosen to continue in your fasting for the supernatural. I have seen your faith and focus. I have released your rewards and I shall never depart from you because you have chosen to stay with me.

As my word says in John 15:7, *"If ye abide in me, and my words abide in you, ye shall ask what ye will, and it shall be done unto you."*

As Jesus is in me, you are in Him and I'm in you as is the Holy Spirit. I have set you up to always win and never to be bound in sin.

I have blinded the enemy. All weapons formed against you have been destroyed. I'm the Lord your God that has done for you. As I did in 2 Chronicles 20:17-25, I have destroyed your enemies and given you their riches. Stand strong and still know that I'm your God and I will never leave or forsake you even until the end.

I'm your friend and you are my beloved. I lay down my life for you, so stay focused on me in all you do. Always know I'm right here with you. It's already done. You have won because of my Son. Enjoy!!!

April 23@4:32 PM

I have covered you. Stay in agreement with your spouse. Speak the same language at all times. Know what's on my mind. There is nothing I won't do for you when you do these things. I have done it all for you.

Don't miss out listening and communicating with people that don't love and respect your spouse or my commandments. If they're not listening to me, they won't listen to you.

Shake the dust off. Continue to do everything I command of you. You will never fail if you obey me. Even conversations from the people you love that are close to you, you can't listen to. They are stuck in traditions and that's the way they have chosen to live.

I brought you out from traditions and old ways. Remember my Word years ago. I have blessed you beyond measure. Don't allow anyone to block what you have the boldness to receive.

The wait is over. It's your time of breakthrough and favor to walk into your seasons. Hear, listen and do what I say to do even when it comes to your close family. Agreement with your spouse is the key to receiving from me, your almighty, all-powerful God.

April 28@9:43 AM

We have moved from the crawling state to the flying state. We have wings like eagles. It's soaring time. No more drought. God has brought us out. Everything that has held us down and shall try to hold us down has been destroyed.

We are raised up by the power of God. We are living from the overflow of the kingdom of God that has been deposited in our house now. Wealth and riches are in our house and never add sorrow. We shall give as the spirit gives us instructions. Men have given unto our bosom.

Our children and children's children are blessed. This is the generation of the righteous. We shall know how to walk in our gifting and callings like never before.

Lay hands on the sick and the sick will be healed. Prophesy and prophecies are revealed and received and the peace of God overrides anything the enemy tries to do. He can't touch you.

You are living under an open heaven. You have the strength of the King and you have received everything, even what the enemy had stolen from you. It's released to you today.

Blessings! Blessings! Blessings are here to stay.

Always remember to do things Gods way. Enjoy! Because you have inherited all the promises of God that have been preserved, provided, and promised you!!!

May 1@9:32 PM

I'm blessed to speak every word that God allows to come out my mouth. My plans and thoughts are established in Christ Jesus. I'm rendering service where service is due. Everything I do is unto You.

You have set me in place and in a position to prosper. My household is blessed and continues to be blessed. God has cut, captured, and canceled all attacks against me, even the most recent ones.

No whores will ever ATTACK my marriage ever again. My husband will never be bound by sin. Grace and mercy is here to stay. Living righteously is always the way. Never give up on God; he will never give up on you. Always do things the way He says do.

People will begin to come to you and ask what must they do for you. Depend on God to speak to them in what to do and what you want them to do. It's all for the kingdom and your house to spill over in their house.

Blessings shall keep on coming, as money will keep on coming to you. Blessings are like a boomerang effect — what you give out is coming back to you in a far greater way than what you gave out.

Your obedience to the seeds sown is the determining factor of your harvest received. Needs have already been meet. Wants and desires have been provided also.

Creative ideas are bursting out of you in ways you couldn't have imagined. The Holy Spirit has revealed these to you. These witty inventions are all to prosper you.

People will buy in record numbers, even when they didn't want to, because of your stretch and sacrifice. Weeds you have received from the supernatural harvest! Get ready — supernatural prosperity is here, and here to stay. Money is on the way NOW!!! Enjoy!!!

May 4@9:21 AM

No more silent or Sleeping Spirit, but a Speaking Spirit. Your spirit must come alive in Christ Jesus. When your spirit is alive, your soul wakes up in the things of God. I'm living in bountiful breakthroughs in every area of my life. I'm living in the overflow outpouring and overtaking of God's manifold, many blessings.

Now, the enemy's hands are tied, will never loose. His eyes are blinded, never to see you because you are hidden in Christ Jesus, under God's almighty wings in His secret pavilion. Even though he seeks and searches, he's not permitted to see you.

God has made you to see from the inside out. You are seeing from the inside of Jesus. You see the enemy when he's trying to see you. God won't allow him to see you as long as you stay hidden in Him. Your sight is very keen and allows you to know what the word of God means.

Keep praying, praising, worshiping, preaching, prophesying, and speaking the Word. Sowing and seeding for Jesus pleases God as He prospers you.

Continue to hear, listen, and do what He speaks to you through the Holy Spirit. God will never leave or forsake you. You should never leave or sake Him. Keep the eyes of your mind on Him at all times. Everything that God has is mine.

May 5@7:57 AM

Keep praising God in all that we do. Praise belongs to you. When we praise God, He adds to His church daily those who will be saved. Keep surrendering to praise, prayer and walking in power. Always continue in right, standing with our God. He's almighty all powerful graceful and full of glory.

He's the reason we can tell our story of how He brought us out of darkness into His marvelous light. As darkness had to be present in order for light to come, in the beginning the victory was won because of His Son. It's already done.

Never stop believing in and trusting in God. You will always go far — as far as the heavens are from the earth, that's how far our blessings reach. No one knows the distance, only know that we are destined to receive from Him.

Wind keeps blowing God keeps showing as we are knowing how to walk in the ways of our God. What we couldn't see is now made available to see and receive. We have a faith that we can see Now!

Because your faith is alive in Christ Jesus, the substance of things and hope and the evidence of things not seen is manifested and released today. No more waiting. The wait is over. It's your time to walk in the manifold seasons of God.

As season come throughout the year, you shall receive year after year never-ending miracles and money. Marriage ministry and mind shall continue to stay focused in Christ Jesus. You have favor from God as you continue in faith and walking in the ways wisdom and word of God!

May 5@10:51 AM

I've given you the land. I've placed it all in your hands. You shall continue to stand. UPE Designs have made you rich and wealthy. I've given you this business to have dominion, be fruitful, multiply, replenish, and subdue, and know that I've done it all for you.

I know I can trust you with money. You had little but continue to sow much. I've taken that seed from the heart and given you more money than you could have ever imagined. This money will never depart, as long as you continue sowing in obedience to me, your almighty, all-powerful God. What comes from your heart reaches my heart.

Customers are coming from all across the world to purchase your designs. They have found you because you have made UPE Designs available to be found. Prepare for the increase. Get ready; money is released. You have running over paying customers.

Never discount what I have given you dominion over. The cattle on a thousand hills are yours. Cattle come in herds; they must stay together. Walk together in the same direction, and so shall you and your spouse. Never allow distractions.

I've blessed the agreement and the fruit of your hands. Your creative ideas and witty inventions shall been seen by the world. Customers will refer others to see what awesome designs you have made. They will know only God could have allowed these magnificent creations to come forth.

You have come from the back to the front. Your website has been seen by the right people to give you favor from God. Investments have come forth. You have extra large seeds to sow from UPE Designs that you didn't even know. Prepare your work area; you need lots of room to flow.

You will hire those I have sent to you. You will know who I send because the Holy Spirit will reveal them to you. Get ready! Get ready! Get ready! I've blessed your hands.

As I told you in the beginning when UPE Designs was birthed. Give her of the fruit of her hands; and let her own works praise her in the gates. (Proverbs 31:31 KJV) you are precious and shall create precious designs to the world.

People shall see that this is the Lord's doing; it's marvelous in our sights. It's not by your might or power but by My Spirit, says the Lord.

My word never returns void; it shall accomplish what I speak and prosper where I send it. Always know I have made this happen for you. Money shall keep on coming to you. You shall always know what to do. Give only to those I say give to.

Continue praying in Holy Spirit, as he reveals all things to you; and he will show you how to walk in them. Never a day goes by without hearing, listening, and doing everything I have said and continue to say to you.

Enjoy it's yours for the asking: and everything you have asked and continue to ask according to my will it's done unto you. I keep my Word! I'm not a man, and I can't lie. Your marriage, money and ministry are prospering NOW!!! Again enjoy. It's my pleasure to prosper you!!!

May 7@9:51 AM

I've seen it on the canvas of my imagination now I'm receiving manifestation — from mind time to manifestation time. You are not a slave to debt. All your needs are met. Never go back to where you have been delivered from.

Concentrate on supernatural debt cancelation and supernatural increase, which will never cease. Continue to hear from me. Don't allow little money to stop you from receiving the big money. Money shall continue to come to you when you follow me. Obey my commands at all times especially with money.

The kingdom is in need and I have blessed you indeed. I've enlarged your territory and my hand is in you. Make sure you continue to do as I say to do. You must owe no man anything. The vows you have made must be paid. You can't pay the debt you owe with other debt owed.

Being free from debt is paying cash and not with credit card. Paying with credit cards will always keep you with a balance and interest. My supernatural debt cancelation doesn't come with balances. The debt has been paid. Increase is staying debt free. Carrying credit cards is carrying balances, which you have been set free from. The price has been paid through Christ Jesus. Enjoy!!!

May 19@9:37 AM

The trigger has been pulled and the bullets have been released. Bullets have power to wound or kill. The bullets I have sent forth shall live and not die. I shall not die, but live, and declare the works of the Lord. (Psalms 118:17)

But he was wounded for our transgressions; he was bruised for our iniquities: the chastisement of our peace was upon him; and with his stripes we are healed. (Isaiah 53:5)

You have power over the enemy. Behold, I give unto you power to tread on serpents and scorpions, and over all the power of the enemy: and nothing shall by any means hurt you. (Luke 10:19 KJV)

I have opened up the lanes for you. Bullets have speed. You have made it to your many destinations quickly sudden right NOW. Speak my word, which never returns void. It accomplishes what I please and prospers where I sent it to.

The enemy can't stop you. So shall my word be that goeth forth out of my mouth: it shall not return unto me void, but it shall accomplish that which I please, and it shall prosper in the thing whereto I sent it. (Isaiah 55:11 KJV)

Why do you think you are not the gun, however the bullets? Because bullets have more power than guns. You see the effects of them. Without the bullets, the gun is of no effect.

Remember, I have made you to be strong in me and in my power. Finally, my brethren, be strong in the Lord and in the power of His might. Put on the whole armor of God that ye may be able to stand against the wiles of the devil. (Ephesians 6:10-11 KJV) This why you are made to be bullets.

I have released my power in you and into this earth, which is mine, and I have given it to you. Enjoy the fullness fruitfulness and fatness of this fertile land that flows with milk and honey and plenty, plenty, plenty of money. That's manifested motivated and has moved into your hands. My kingdom has wealth because you have wealth.

Continue to walk in right standing with me, your almighty, all-powerful God. You will never lack or be in want. The young lions do lack and suffer hunger: but they that seek the Lord shall not want any good thing. (Psalms 34:10 KJV)

May 19@9:40 AM

Never be settled with where you have been. You are made with a purpose you are chosen for a purpose be fruitful multiply subdue replenish because I have given you dominion right here on earth. The earth is the Lords and the fullness there of. Walk in victory. Come to me with nakedness, laying aside every weighty sin that's so easily beset you.

Praise me in all you do. I've made this all happen for you. In all you do, stay focused in faith. I've made a way even when you couldn't see a way. Don't sweat the small things in life; you have the finer things in life — this life and life more abundantly. Work the process and plans that been set up for you to progress.

Remember the cross experience. I've given my only begotten son. The victory has been won. It's yours for the asking. Everything you have asked of me according to my will I've given you. Continue to worship me in spirit and in truth. I never leave or forsake you. I love you. It's my pleasure prosper you. You are blessed going in and blessed coming out. You are blessed in the cities and blessed in the fields.

I've opened up the white fields of harvest, which is plenteous for you. Walk in my perfect will for your life. You are out — shout, because the walls are down. I shall always be around in your life. All your needs I have meet. All your desires are my desires for you.

Again, stay in you lane that I've opened up for you. Continue in the race that I set you in. Don't get off track. You are moving in the right direction that I've divinely instructed you to follow. You shall make it to your destination. Continue to walk in my love.

Decree and declare my Word regardless to what people say. Don't allow them to rise against you while I'm allowing the Holy Spirit to speak my Word through you. It's my Word that controls the situations that people face. They shall hear what I have to say.

I've set up another place for you to Sheppard over…lead the sheep feed the sheep never sleep with the sheep never do it your way again or manipulate the sheep. You have been chastised. You have arrived to higher heights and always look to the hills from which has come your help. Lean on and rely on and trust my help.

Blessings, favor, grace, and mercy only come from me. You can't make happen what I've allowed to die. You are dead to sin and alive in me. I'm your almighty, all-powerful God. You are beloved. I've given you the world and all that's in it. Enjoy!!!

May 23@7:22 AM
Personal for Lady Mary! Happy Birthday from God!

Today is my day for my miracles. I receive my miracles today. Blessings are moving my way. Blessings are here to stay.

UPE Designs is on customers' minds and they purchase at all times. Customers have found UPE Designs. Customers are attracted to attached and attacking UPE Designs NOW!

My designs are created beautifully and are pleasing to the eyes of the beholders. Customers are purchasing UPE Designs all across this world. They are downloading *Things Seen In The Spirit* by the hundreds of thousands.

I'm shouting because I'm out. No more debt. All my needs are met. I have plenty more to put in store. My savings account is overflowing.

I'm sowing seeds like never before. Supernatural increase and debt cancelation is knocking at my door. I've opened the doors and I'm walking in my supernatural increase and debt cancelation. The spirit of the Lord is on me.

My eyes are opened now; I can see. Everything that God has for me; it's bigger than I could have ever imagined. I have been set in this large place because of God's grace. I have unmerited favor from God and man. Wealth and riches are in my hands. I receive all God that has for me.

The blessings of the Lord are on me. I have been made a God-made miracle millionaire. I have what I desire to have. I wear what I desire to wear. I go where I desire to go. I drive what I desire to drive. I eat what I desire to eat. I'm blessed beyond measure. I've received from heaven. I can't explain how it all happened. I just trusted and believed. God promised it all in His Word.

I shall stay faithful available and teachable, as my Apostle Dr. Leroy Thompson told me. God has given seed to me because I'm obedient to sow. This is a commandment from God I know. Seed time is always connected to harvest time.

I have the prayer of prophecy on me. Souls will be saved when I speak. Lives will change when I speak. Money will come when I speak. Miracles will happen when I speak. Love will override hate when I speak. Supernatural healing will happen when I speak. Supernatural deliverance will happen when I speak. Supernatural harvest and breakthroughs will happen when I speak. All because of the spirit of the Lord is upon me.

I see what God wants me to see, and I'm all He wants me to be. I'm relaxed, rested, rendering, receiving revelations, and releasing revealed secrets from my almighty, all-powerful God. He has set me apart and made me holy, as He is holy.

I shall stay in the lane God has opened up for me to travel in. I will never be bound by sin. There are paths that have been set up particularly for me to travel through. There are doors that have been opened particularly for me to enter in.

God has set destinations for me to reach. I reach and I receive all destinations that God has divinely directed for me, all because I hear listen and do as He instructs me to. This comes by being willing obedient and serving God as He has called and commanded me to be one of His servants. The overtaking outpouring of blessings and miracles are on me Now! And men shall give unto me Now! I believe I have received and I'm walking in miracles Now! And I thank God for it all.

June 3@6:33 AM

I receive I receive I receive the blessings of the lord is on me! I'm anointed to prosper the oil is in my hands. Everything I touch stands. Gold is released to me. Grace is released to me. God's power is released on me. Everything that I dreamed of and imagined and couldn't have imagined is mine. It's my time. Quickly suddenly! I have received my manifested release.

Breakthroughs are here. Bountiful blessings are here. Money just keeps on coming to you now. UPE Designs is on people's minds. They are purchasing plenty of products and prospering you. Remember seed time and harvest time because the blessings of the Lord are on you your household, family, and friends. They are blessed because of the connection to you. Remember your connections because you are blessed because of the blessings that's on them.

Don't sweat the small stuff because I've set you in a large place far greater than what you see right now. The wealth of the wicked is yours now. Wealth and riches are in your house. This is their final destination. Wealth and riches have set up residence in your house and have made your house a home. You have begun to see the unknown unseen hidden treasures that's been laid up and promised you now! I receive! I receive! I receive all my bountiful blessing and breakthroughs in every area of my life.

Money has come to me today. Miracles have manifested to me today. I'm moving into new ministries today. I have no stress, struggles or strain because I'm in God's van and He has opened up the lanes.

I'm anointed to prosper everything I touch prospers. Everything I speak according to God's word comes to pass. The blessings are coming fast and they always last. Never ending unmovable unlimited blessings are coming quickly sudden right now. I'm the God of all in all and in Christ Jesus you will never fall. You are ready to receive the blessings of the lord is on me. Thank you God for all you have given me.

June 5@6:55 AM

Sound Wisdom
Supernatural Wealth
Saturated Word
Solid Witness

These things I speak to you to do. I have given you my Word and you know what to do. You are my witness in every part of the earth. Go when and where I say go. The nations are in place to hear you. You shall work while it's day, night comes to no man who can work.

You are willing and obedient and eating the good of the land. You are obeying and serving me therefore you are spending your days in prosperity and your years in pleasure. It's my pleasure to prosper you. Stay built up in my Word; it never fails in anything I set it up to do.

The lost shall be found by the words of your mouth; don't be afraid shout it out. Tell my people they are rich beyond measure. No one can put a price on their money and ministry. Jesus paid it all. He is the one the blessings are flowing through. In Christ Jesus all your needs are meet and you have my Supernatural Wealth and Sound Wisdom. Always stay Saturated in my Word because you are a Solid Witness.

Take heed to these saying I give you. I speak to you this way for you to understand what I say. You shall receive more and more every day. My Revelations, Riches, and Rest are Reigning in your life NOW! Never discount, discredit, disconnect from the people I've placed and positioned in your life to help you receive all my favor that I have promised you. Never give up on me as I allow you to continue to speak. You have my word on it.

No devil can take my Word from you. You know exactly what to do. Stay focus and in faith. Your finances are on the way and they are here to stay. Expect exceedingly abundantly efficiently money that does will always abound in your life. This is my will and you have my Word on it. Enjoy NOW!!!

June 6@7:24 AM

Pop goes the weasel — you have been released out of the box. Released from poverty into prosperity. Released from sickness and into health and wholeness. Moving from disturbance and depression into peace. Released from debt into supernatural increase.

The spirit of the Lord is upon you. Spread your wings; you are about to sing of all God's greatness and His awesome works and power.

People are about to come to your ministries both near and far. Your new church family has been set up for you to function in all God wants you to do. You are the Pastors of 10,000 members. This includes your local church family and the families across the nations. Your travels begin now! Get your itinerary ready and clear your schedule.

Get in shape exercise your faith. You will need to be in great shape. People are ready to be healed, delivered, and set free.

Money has come to me. Money just keeps on coming to me. You shall have plenty money for the kingdom's sake. Make no mistake, wealth and riches are released in your house. That's why you are out of the box — pop goes the weasel is a saying of the world.

I take the foolish things of the world and use for the wise — popping is a quickening release. That's why I said, "Pop goes the weasel."

Things shall happen quickly, suddenly, right now! Get ready because the task is great. It's all for my name's sake. Jesus is being released into the hearts and minds of the people who have been crying and calling out to me. I've chosen commanded and commission you to bring them in and out of the world of sin.

Teach my people. Train my people to always trust me, as you stay faithful to me. Remember, these are my people and not yours. Sheep need to be led and fed, not to be in your bed. Keep these words in your heart always. Never lead the sheep astray.

I'm trusting you. I'm trusting you with my kingdom as I've given you dominion. As my Word says in Genesis, the whole chapter one, whatever YOU call it that's what it will be. The control you have has come from me. Get this key verse down in your spirit. And God blessed them, and God said unto them, Be fruitful, and multiply, and replenish the earth, and subdue it: and have dominion over the fish of the sea, and over the fowl of the air, and over every living thing that moveth upon the earth. (Genesis 1:28 KJV)

Shout because you're out, and the nations are coming out as well. Go bare and bring fruit into the bountiful blessings that I've prepared and promised to them. As I have placed and positioned you for this awesome work, stay in agreement speak the same language remain faithful. Stay in the driver's seat; you've got the wheel. It's your job to bring souls in.

In Christ Jesus you shall always win. Never be bound by sin. Again, it's for my name's sake. I'm your almighty, all-powerful God. I make no mistake. As you are made in my image so was Jesus.

Do everything as unto me. I've set you in a large place you are on display. You are on your way, getting going. You know what to do. The lane is wide-open for you. Enjoy the ride!!! I'm always by your side. Receive! Receive! Receive!!!

June 6@7:34 AM

You are greater than where you're living. That is your life in Christ Jesus. Your heart must be in total connection with God Jesus and Holy Spirit. The angels are working for you to continue the contract that God has set up for you.

Don't be deceive and allow the enemy to trick trap and tempt you into denying and destroying the finish work of Christ Jesus. It's already designed and divinely delivered to you accept what God has set up for you. This is His will for you. Enjoy the promotions and prosperity from God because it pleases Him to prosper you…don't give up because of what you see right now it's temporary light afflictions and the eternal is a moment away God's blessings are here to stay! Enjoy!!!

June 6@8:09 AM

When you stand straight up with your hands extended out from side by side, that's an example of a picture of the cross. I worship you, God, for the cross experience you allowed Jesus to die for me and rise up again for my sins. He paid the price, now I pay you back with my worship. I see what Jesus sees. I'm made in your image.

I imagine the things from you God. I have inspiration, impartation, and instructions from you God. When I stretch out my hands, I'm extending my worship to you, Lord. Worship is what I know and choose to do. It's the way I live.

I give praise to you with my whole heart you make me the full branch. I bare much fruit because you have purged me and pruned me to be just like you. I'm an expression of your goodness greatness and giving spirit. I worship you in spirit and in truth I thank you for seeking me out to worship you. I'm your true worshipper.

I stand when no one else will stand. I stand because everything you got is in my hands. You have given me the fullness of this earth. You've given me dominion and I have received it. Oh, how wonderful are the works of Jesus. I praise you, God, for your Son. Because of him, the victory is won.

I will never take worship for granted. I will praise you from the rising of the sun until the going down of the same. I will bless your holy name, for your goodness and your mercy towards me. As the spirit of the Lord is on me, I get up I go into my place of worship daily. I never forget to thank you, God, as worship comes from my heart. Worship and I shall never depart.

This is my inward praise. What You have placed on the inside of me, I give back to you. My mind, body, and soul. I let the world know who You are and what you have done and are still doing because of Your Son. I'm your beloved that You first loved. Now I'm giving back to You the love You've given me.

My worship is my words from You. I praise You in all I do. I give You glory, Lord, in my praise as I worship You now and always.

June 8@7:09 AM

I'm picked out for a purpose. I serve the purposed and plan that God has set in place for me. I remember that the price has been paid. I'm never bound with the mistakes that I've made. I stay in the lane that God has opened up for me and I do this by always following His agenda. I'm the righteousness of God. God is my father. I'm His beloved child. I go the extra mile.

Seasons come and seasons go. I will always sow. I'm blessed in every season. I have reserves even in off seasons. I'm always living in my seasons of breakthrough favor from my almighty, all-powerful God. I never count my blessings because there are no endings to my blessings. They continue to come because the victory has been won, all because of His Son.

I'm never weary and weeping in well doing, however I'm reaping and fainting not. I'm always grateful for what I got. As tough times come, I will never give up on God because He will never give up on me.

I don't concentrate on the things that I see that are not going right for me. I'm in faith and believing what God has in His plan for me. I follow and receive His instructions and know what to do.

My gifts and talents will always make room for me and I finish the work that I've been called to. I stay away from negative naysayers. Their conversations aren't fit for me. God has sent many people for me to meet and greet and He has many destinations for me to see. I never get off track with conversations that hold me back. I move forward I keep pressing as I have already learned my lesson in the testing.

God's Son is the prize and God is the prize-giver. He gives to whom He please, as I remember who blesses me. God is my source and strength. He's the light when there is no light. God speaks what He wants and means what He says.

I'm assured that blessings have come my way and they are here to stay as I always do things His way. I reap the harvest that's plenteous and I'm one of the chosen few. God has put me in Remembrance of His Word that says, "But thou shalt remember the Lord thy God: for it is he that giveth thee power to get wealth that he may establish His covenant which he sware unto thy fathers, as it is this day." (Deuteronomy 8:18 KJV)

I hear, listen, and do what He says as I know that He has sent blessings my way and I will never lack another day.

June 9@7:51 AM

When debt is released that our fortune can increase. We have plenty more to put in store. God has opened doors, the ones we know of and the one we know not of. Drop your line; it's your time. The fish are overloading the net, so much so that the net will break. The souls have come in, the kingdom wins.

You never have to think about where money is coming from again. You are rich and wealthy and this is my pleasure. Stay calm in the storm it won't last, because this too shall pass. God shall always bring it to full manifestation in your favor.

Favor and finances has come to you now! No more lack; never look back. Receive your supernatural multiplied miracle and manifested money in my hands now! The transactions has been made and deposited into my account. You have a money flow; it's flooding and flourishing to you now! Enjoy!

June 20@6:01 AM

Who's pulling your string? You're not a puppet. Don't let people shake you or pull you into their way of life. The puppet has a string attached and someone had to attach the string. Make sure you are the originator of the string and you control the string.

Abundance is our birthright. Never let the enemy break you. You have bountiful blessings that have been released to you. And God said, Let us make man in our image, after our likeness: and let them have dominion over the fish of the sea, and over the fowl of the air, and over the cattle, and over all the earth, and over every creeping thing that creepeth upon the earth. So God created man in His own image, in the image of God created he him; male and female created he them. And God blessed them, and God said unto them, be fruitful, and multiply, and replenish the earth, and subdue it: and have dominion over the fish of the sea, and over the fowl of the air, and over every living thing that moveth upon the earth. (Genesis 1:26-28 KJV)

The earth is the Lord's, and the fullness thereof; the world, and they that dwell therein. (Psalms 24:1 KJV)

June 20@6:01 AM

If you're going to be Powerful and Pleasing in God sight and Produce the results that God wants, you can't be a puppet on the string and let people pull you here and there and every where. Remember, a puppet has a master who attaches the string. You have a God who is your master and allows you to attach the string — the string of Prayer, Praise, Preaching, being Prophetic — which allows Him to release Promises, Promotions, and Prosperity.

As believers we must control the string attached to the puppet. Pull people into the kingdom of God. Go after the lost that want to be found. People do what they want to do. If they don't want to be healed, delivered, set free from sin, they will stay in bondage. They commit adultery because they want to. They're not going to jump off a cliff. They know that they will die, and it's their own fault if they chose to jump.

Don't let people tell you it's your fault that they did what they did — cheating or whatever it is they did, adultery lying, etc.

They think they won't get caught but God sees all and knows all (believers) and reveals to all who asks. And whatsoever ye shall ask in my name, that will I do, that the Father may be glorified in the Son. If ye shall ask any thing in my name, I will do it. (John 14:13-14 KJV)

June 20@7:03 AM

Crown of Glory, this is my story. People will see the glory of the Lord in you. I'm crowned with glory and majesty. I've placed my glory and majestic presence on you. My glory is revealed and released through you. You shall always know what to do.

Never be seen for your own works, know that it's I your almighty, all-powerful God that works through you and the works that you do come from me. Never work for you always work for me. The world calls itself employed; I call your works supernatural endowment. This is my ever-increasing, everlasting always doing the work of the Lord.

Always let your light shine so I can be seen in you. Never allow your lamp to be hidden under the things of the world, which I've not told you to do. The world didn't make you as well as you didn't make you.

Don't try to be seen for your works, allow the works that I've established in you to come forth. If you do this you shall always come forth as pure gold ... with no imitation, however information instructions and inspiration from me. It's glory time and story time, to tell of your testimonies I've given you. The light is brightly shinning and everything is unwinding.

The wind of wealth has blown in. Receive from me because of the things you have been in. The fight is over and you can tell your story. You have my crown of glory. This crown that I have fixed upon you and the enemy don't know what to do. This crowns that shinning so bright because you have won the fight. The wait is over it's your time.

Everything that the lord owns is mine. Sudden quickly it's here. Receive of the lord rest in Him always. The power of God is resting on you and you always know what to do. Again, I've made it all happen for you. Enjoy!

June 25@9:43 PM

Souls just keep on coming. You have asked them to come from the north, south, east, and west. I've given you the best crops. Harvest of souls is here, solely because I'm near.

You are seeing what you call shortages today; however this is your holding pattern. Trust me for the supernatural zone, by obeying me with your tithes and offering. I've provided and made a way of escape, which is your giving.

I've given you seeds to sow however the tithes are what you owe. Never look at your circumstances because they are temporary light afflictions only for a moment ... so quick you won't know they existed if you resist it. It being the thoughts of what you don't have today. Theirs is more and more on the way, when you do what I say.

Next week all doors and windows are opening. You will walk in. It's no surprise because I've allowed you to rise. You shall reach higher heights. It's soaring time as I've told you before. Enter into my place of prosperity and peace because pleases me. Give me the tithes and watch me provide.

I have people waiting on you to do what I say do. I can't release what you haven't released. Open your hands and your heart so you can receive your harvest. Never be afraid to give me my money; it doesn't belong to you.

The tenth is cursed in your hands and blessed in my hands. I bless the ninety percent, I rebuke the devourer for your sakes. I allow meat to be and stay in your house. So open your hands and let it out. Shout because you are out. This is the way money shall keep on coming to you.

Start looking for your harvest, preparing and expecting it. I have arrived at your house, standing, and knocking waiting to come in. I know you will obey and let me in because I've allowed you to win.

June 27@6:30 AM

The glory of the Lord is here. I see white clouds. The white fields are already harvested. Your riches are the process of the state of being wealthy and possession of your wealth. You have and are in possession of wealth you have to know how to hear from God. Listen and do in order to get the wealth to you.

Take the steps and walk in wealth. Move into what I've provided for you. You know what to do. The plans are laid out for you. Follow my instructions that I've already imparted in you.

You have my Word. Continue in my Word daily. Never have down time from my Word. Never go a day without hearing, listening and obeying me. Continuing is the key to me. Your almighty, all-powerful God.

You are my prayer warrior, PRAISER preacher, and prophet. I put praise in the middle because when you pray first, you open up heaven and begin to praise me to bring the preacher and prophetic forth. My Word is key to prayer, praise, preacher, and prophet.

When you pray, speak my Word. When you praise, speak my Word. When you preach, speak my Word. When you prophesy, speak my Word.

In all you do, always stay focused in faith and I shall bring fruit and finances even in the day of famine you shall be filled, full, flooded, and fat, with the good of the land. It's all in my plan. I make no mistake I made it all this way for you to work while it's day because when the end comes, no man can work.

You are my workmanship, chosen, called, commissioned, and commanded to go, not sit back and wait for me to do it all for you. Now get up get going. You will receive better bountiful blessings like never before. It's all in store. I've preserved promised and provided your prosperity and it's my pleasure to give it to you. Enjoy!!!

June 30@11:14 PM

This Thursday sees doors and windows opening, and I will walk in. I'm walking in my seasons. I've made it by the grace of God. God favored me. Here I am to worship You, God. I bow down and worship you, Lord. I live to worship You. I worship You; I live.

Giving is my life and my life is blessed because I give. I am a God-made miracle millionaire. I have no debt because Jesus paid it all for me. I'm walking in the favor, fruitfulness, and finances of God. He keeps on blessing me over and over again.

God allows me to always win. Every day I wake up I know I have the victory. Victory is mine. I'm never in doubt. I'm shouting because God has brought me out.

Wealth and health is my birthright. God gave it me in the beginning and He will never take it away. The blessings of the Lord are upon me. I'm debt free. I have no stress, no struggle, no strain; God has allowed it to reign.

I'm receiving manna from heaven. I receive my breakthroughs in every area of my life. I'm walking in the supernatural surplus. I'm receiving and resting in God's promises, provisions, promotions, peace, and prosperity. It's all directed divinely and delivered to me.

I love this life I'm living. I have received it all while in the Spirit. My natural man enjoys the pleasures of God from the spirit man. Everything God owns I own because I'm made in His image. I receive my wealth and riches now and forever more.

I walk through the doors that God has opened for me. I receive the wind of wealth that's has been blown in from the windows that have been opened for me.

July 26@1:14 PM

God allows me to be that bridge for my family, friends, and faithful to cross over. I'm the model, mentor, motivator and I've been placed on this Mantle for the entire world to see. The spirit of the Lord is upon me. I shall live life according to God's standards and statues, as I'm stationed, solid and standing strong, sustained in the supernatural surplus of almighty, all-powerful God. He wishes above all things that I prosper be in health even my soul prospers.

Every part of my life lives according to the will, ways, wisdom, Word and wealth of God. Satan is defeated. My life is completed in CHRIST Jesus. I live, wear, and drive the best. I live a first class lifestyle. People shall know who I am and whose I am. I have been placed in what people call the Hall of Fame. Everyone shall know my name.

God calls this place the Heart of Faith. Where God has made a way out of no way. Testimonies have been birthed for all to see on earth. The Hall of Fame lists people's names for their great work on earth in their particular field. The Heart of Faith has God's people's names because of their belief in Him and continual work for Him, regardless of the situations that try to stop them.

These people believe in God and the work He has done and shall continue to do and grafter works He allows us to do. Their hearts are like gold and the testimonies are told. These people are purified and have the Holy Ghost fire that can't be put out. It's a continual fire than never burns out and no one can contain it. This fire spreads; anyone near this Holy Ghost fire, it will attach and attract to them.

Hall of Fame people remember them and some don't. Heart of Faith God allows His people to never want. When God calls your name and writes your name in His Heart of Faith, your name shall always be great. Because His name is the name above all names and His name remains the same. As you are in His image so as He, so are you. Remember to hear, listen, and always do everything as He says to do. He shall continue to make it happen for you.

July 26@1:32 PM

Jesus Plus Veins

I'm functioning in the veins of Jesus. Without the functioning of veins, there will be no flow of blood. The veins are designed to house the blood. The blood of Jesus saved us from death, destruction, and devastation. The blood of Jesus has delivered us from the hands of the enemy. The blood of Jesus has washed away our sins and made us whole again. I'm living life through the blood in Christ Jesus, our Lord and saviour.

I'm aware and awake to my behavior. I see life through the blood of Jesus. Because of the blood, I'm walking in my season. Seasons come and go, however the blood continues to flow.

In my veins the blood reigns and remains. Through the functioning and flowing of my blood in my veins, my life will never be the same. The veins are connected to other organs and parts of my body, as Jesus is connected to the father.

I shall forever be connected to Jesus. I'm alive because of this reason. Without the blood in my veins my life won't be sustained. Without the blood of Jesus, I'm living this life in vain. With the blood of Jesus all things remain.

With the blood in my veins, my life remains. Thank you God for the blood of Jesus and the blood functioning and flowing in my veins.

July 28@10:45 PM

Bells and Whistles

Signs and Wonders

These are warnings and signs letting you know something is about to happen — things to come, signs and wonders. Get ready for the blessings and to be a blessing. God has arrived at your house, pouring you out blessings. You won't have enough room to receive.

When you hear the Word of God, shout because you are out. No more poverty but plenty of prosperity. No more lack but life, and life more abundantly; more than enough for the kingdom of God and more than enough for your house. God has already laid it out and up for you receive from your obedience, hearing, listening and doing what His Holy Spirit speaks to and through you.

Receive God's wisdom, Word, and wealth, which is in your house. The alarm has been sounded. The whistle has been blown. You shall receive wealth unknown. These are the signs and wonders I've made for you in particular to see — for your eyes only.

These are the times and seasons of your breakthrough. Favor comes from labor to favor. I command you this day to receive your blessings because I've made you a blessing. You can't be a blessing without these blessings. This is my will for you receive, receive, receive!

You have passed the need and come into the seeds. Your crops have come up and continue to grow as you continue to sow. These things I give you that you didn't know. Stay in your row; it's been dug up and seeded for you. This is my pleasure to prosper you!

July 29@7:40 AM

Spread your wings. The glory of the Lord is here. He's in the atmosphere. He's always near. You are flying to higher heights. You are moving fast. Don't come down. You will never stop what you started in me. I put the plan in motion. Move, move! I have approved.

Every place that the soles of your feet have treaded upon, it's yours for the asking. You are moving. It's my will for you to prosper. I'm pleased to prosper you. Continue, continue.

Never be settled with little; little isn't in my plan. Abundant is your birthright. Dominion in the beginning; dominion in the ending. You shall reach the nations. People will come from the north, south, east, and west. I've given you my very best.

Money is released for the kingdom's sake. Money is released for my sake. You have wealth and riches in your house. I've brought you out. Shout, shout!

Checks are in the mail. Supernatural money has been deposited into your account. It's not a mistake. It's for the kingdom's sake, my sake, and your sake.

Don't allow the little leaven; leaven the whole lump. Don't put anything in that you don't want to come out. A little alcohol, a little drug — no one will know. Wrong, I know. I need you clean and clear. Your time is here. Don't spoil the supernatural surplus.

Things are rotten if you leave them there or do things outside of my will. Righteousness I've given to you. I've made you this way. Flow, flourish, flood in my finances.

Stop the private little moments with the enemy. Letting him tell you it's all right, it's okay to do it this way. A little drink and drugging won't hurt and won't be seen. I reveal expose and remove. Don't miss my move. Continue to move, move. Spread your wings. I've given you everything. Enjoy!

August 5@9:19 AM

Can God trust you to trust Him? God is faithful in covenants and commandments. His agreements and doing what He says do, regardless of what you want to do. You trust God and can God trust you to trust Him.

In (Duet 7:9) it says in the middle of the verse, with them that love Him. When you are in covenant with God you can't make a covenant outside of God. He doesn't make any side contracts. He's the only source, but He gives you resources.

People who disrespect the commandments, you shouldn't show them any favor. If you do, God will turn on you because you are disrespecting God when you disrespect His commands.

We must know who God wants us to associate with and do so. We must not cancel out what God has already put in motion. He has allowed money to move, be mounted mightily and be motivated to manifest to us. Don't stop short of God blessings by allowing people that don't obey and love Him to stop you. Receive all that He has promised provided and prospered you with.

We ask God to forgive us for associating with people that don't love, obey, respect, don't agree with Him, and don't do what He says to do. We cancel anything that had stopped and tried to stop us from receiving our wealth and riches that's already in our house.

August 7@9:52 PM
1/14/2015, First spoken by God

MY VISION ... (Revealed Now In Writing, because Apostle said to write down my vision)

Money is in my mouth; it must be spoken out. Money cometh to me now, in Jesus' name. Money with a plan is in my hand and it has come from man, and men give unto my bosom. I have fast-track money, overnight delivery. Checks are in the mail. The seeds are coming in. I always win. Wealth and riches are in my house.

Shout, for the victory is won. I am God's beloved one. Hear the whistling in the wind, I'm blowing them in like a mighty rushing wind.

The property is yours for the kingdom's sake. There will be no stress, struggle or strain. You are in my vain. It's reigning. The harvest is here.

You shall teach reach and preach across this world. You shall pray for the sick and the sick be healed immediately. You shall call money and it cometh NOW!!!

UPE Designs has a continual supernatural money flow. I shall send people to give and help with your business. There will be more money for you and more for the kingdom.

Continue to listen to the sound follow and flow in the rhythm. I shall send the whirlwind of blessings that shall capture and catch you up, and release you into the seven fold manifold manifested release of supernatural debt cancelation and supernatural increase. It is already in my kingdom and in your house:

1) Power

2) Riches

3) Wisdom

4) Honor

5) Strength

6) Glory

7) Blessings

All seven of these I give to you NOW!!! Receive NOW!!! Enjoy!!!

August 9@2:27 AM

It's your time to shine in my divine. Decree and declare and make the people aware that I'm always there. I'm the great, mighty and all-powerful God. I'm never far. I'm closer than ever before.

Open the door of your heart invite me in, this is where I enter in. Never allow anyone or anything to block my entrance. The world say let's wine and dine. I say it's your time to shine in my divine.

No more barrier blockers. It's time to shock and rock. People will say, "Who is this person?" They will see what I can and have done. The victory is won because of my son.

Everything you shall do is in Christ Jesus. Faithfulness in Christ Jesus. Fruitfulness in Christ Jesus. Flourishing in Christ Jesus. Finances in Christ Jesus. Kingdom residence and no more residue. Clean and clear.

You see through the glass of grace, as I give you my goodness and glory. My glory is here in this atmosphere. Don't forget where I brought you from. I've allowed your healing and deliverance to come.

You are saved and set free from everything you've been trying to flee. Walk in my will, wisdom, and Word.

You stayed in the race regardless of the obstacles and obstructions that tried to stop you. You kept the pace. You made it. Continue to seek me daily. Hear, listen, and do as I command you to. Tell your testimony that others will come to know me in a more excellent way. Remember to obey Holy Spirit and know it's all for the kingdom's sake.

August 13@10:55 AM

Regardless of what you think a person is or not doing, God has already done it. Watch the negative words you speak; you can't take them back. Don't listen to negative words others speak; they get inside your mind and come up again. John 16:33 says, These things I have spoken unto you, that in me ye might have peace. In the world ye shall have tribulation: but be of good cheer; I have overcome the world. Death and life is in the power of YOUR tongue not anyone else.

What you speak is from you and what others speak is from them, so no one can speak death on you and God allows it to happen just because they spoke it. You choose the blessings not the curses. Continue to speak what the Holy Spirit speaks through you, not what you want or what others speak for you or to you. Make sure your words build up, not tear down.

Proverbs 4:24 says: Put away from thee a froward mouth, and perverse lips put far from thee.

Proverbs 26:28 MSG says: Liars hate their victims; flatterers sabotage trust.

Titus 3:2 NLT says: They must not slander anyone and must avoid quarreling. Instead, they should be gentle and show true humility to everyone.

Colossians 2:4 AMP: I say this in order that no one may mislead and delude you by plausible and persuasive and attractive arguments and beguiling speech.

Romans 16:17 says: Now I beseech you, brethren, mark them which cause divisions and offenses contrary to the doctrine which ye have learned; and avoid them. God reveals exposes and removes every word spoken any anything done that didn't come from Him when you ask. Ask it shall be given. Seek and you shall find. Knock and the door shall be opened unto you.

This is what Matthew 7:7 NLT says...Keep on asking, and you will receive what you ask for. Keep on seeking, and you will find. Keep on knocking, and the door will be opened to you. This is a continual process to receive continual progress...and all promotions, provisions and prosperity from almighty all-powerful God. He blesses the fruit of your lips with peace and healing.

Isaiah 57:19 says: I create the fruit of the lips; Peace, peace to him that is far off, and to him that is near, saith the Lord; and I will heal him. Never forsake to speak Gods Word in season and out of season. Always have a speaking spirit that only comes from God.

August 18@9:44 PM

I'm in the middle of the WIND. and I always WIN. I've blessed your GOING out and your coming IN. Go in and possess the land; this land where living rivers of water continue to flow, flourish, and flood your banks.

These are the institutions that I give you to deposit my whirlwind of wealth. This wealth that has stationed, staged, and secured and has strict orders from God by way of the Holy Ghost to enter INTO your house. No stopping or stagnation, however straight INTO your bank accounts with no hindrance. No one knows how. Miracles, Miracles, Miracles are yours NOW!!!

Close your mouth; it's not a surprise. I told you I would bring you out. NOW SHOUT!!! The walls of lack are down. The walls of debt are down. The walls of sickness and disease are down. The supernatural surplus is here; it's yours NOW!!! Receive, Receive, Receive!!!

I've meet your needs. Now, you have your manifested release. You have sown sacrificial and stretch seeds from the little you had. I'm making your little to be many and more than enough.

Money and mansions are moving and magnetically mounted to you, never leaving your hands. No more empty hands. You shall never go empty. I've filled your barns and storehouses with plenty. Lack or want, you won't have any. I've positioned you for prosperity.

Your dreams have come to reality. You are seeing and living out your dreams. You are awakened and walking in your best years ever. You have your new church and your new home. You have sought the kingdom first and my righteousness, and I give you the desires of your heart. Enjoy the move.

I know you shall remember me in all you do. Your testimonies have come through. You know what to do. Tell them to those I tell you to.

Because you have obeyed and served me and you stayed faithful to me, I'm pleased for you to live your days in prosperity and your years in pleasure. Enjoy!!!

August 19@10:01 PM

Don't be distracted; the dirt is uncovered and removed. Washed and cleansed by the blood of Jesus, never to be buried or covered up again. Nothing hidden; everything revealed, exposed, and removed.

You never have to wonder or get weary in well doing; you shall reap and faint not. Everything is brought out. The blood keeps and covers you. Continue in my Word. I've imparted and instructed you to increase. As seed time and harvest time never cease. I've laid it all at your feet. Money that's all from me. Your almighty, all-powerful God.

You have entered into my place of rest, restoration, and release. I've given you everything that the enemy thought he could keep from you. You are blessed beyond your dreams. You have *big* dreams. I have even bigger things that you couldn't have even dreamed of or imagined. If you could have dreamed these things, you would have thought they weren't from me, for real or even reachable.

You have monster money. Don't be afraid, it's just my way of explaining how much money has been released to you. I have allowed the billionaires to find you. They know what to do by way of the Holy Spirit. They don't know why they released the monies, they have heard from me. This is my doing. It's marvelous in the sight of all who see.

The Red Sea is open unto you. Go and possess the land. It's all in my plans. I've anointed you to prosper. I can trust you to take care of, teach, and reach the people. Because you have done this blessings shall keep outpouring overflowing and over taking you and your house. Receive, enjoy!!! It's my pleasure.

August 21@7:53 PM

It's my time to unwind in God's divine. Supernatural increase and supernatural debt cancellation is mine. Quickly, like the blinking of an eye. I will not just get by. My money is made to multiply. I'm the apple of God's eye.

I'm spreading my wings. I've learned how to fly. It's soaring time. Higher and higher; I won't come down. God has shut the door. I can never ever be poor. I enter into my place and position of wealth. All God's promises He has kept.

No more weary, weeping or wondering; I have the wisdom and power to get my wealth. All the shelves are swept clean. Resources, resources, I have the means. No more shortages. All my money is fat, full, fruitful, flowing, flooding, and flourishing. Deeper and deeper the treasure chest of Heaven is wide open. No more doubt.

It's drinking time. Shout because we are out. By God's will, we'll never run dry; we have a continual flow. Sow, sow, sow, this is how it all happened, I know.

My spirit is rich and receiving all revelations from God. My spirit, soul, mind, and heart obey God. Blessings, blessings, and blessings never depart. Receive, receive, and receive, I have no need, but increase, increase, and increase. It's all for me. Enjoy!!!

August 25@2:51 AM

Upload and download your blessings. They are set in the process, programmed, and promised frame. I've framed your photos and completed your app before you knew there was one. I'm allowing your special image to be seen. Show yourself. I've given you help. Handle with care, caution, and compassion; this is your continual progress.

See yourself on the banner of belief. All things have been made possible to you. There's nothing impossible from me, as I give you all things designed especially for you. You are wrapped in wisdom, wealth, and my Word. You are clothed in righteousness.

Watch me continue to do a work in you. Nothing can and will be able to stop you. Look, leap, and launch. The ships have come in. You have made it to the other side. This is the side of pleasure, peace, protection, promotion, and prosperity.

The fish have come in. Because of your faithfulness you will always win. Receive your manna from heaven. It's my pleasure to give you the treasure. Open the box; it's not locked.

You are loaded with money. Money COMETH to you now. Speak money break out. From the east, west, north, and even the south. Money is spoken out. Money just keeps on coming out, there's no more drought. Overflow, overflow, overflow! Let the blessings flow. I did this for you and all the world shall know. Don't stop telling of my wonderful works. Receive, receive, and receive all my increase. Enjoy!!!

August 27@8:40 PM

If you are filled with the Holy Spirit, you must obey the Holy Spirit. Do what He says. If the Holy Spirit is in you, you will not continue to do what you want to do or what the enemy speaks to you. Example lack, lying, being unfulfilled, and suffering unfaithfulness: such as men that choose to live, lay and lie in adultery and make themselves think it's not a sin. They disobey God, who warns them against it. If you look at and lust after a woman you will hear God's voice and know which way to go or what to do.

The Holy Spirit gives you evidence and encouragement. He gives you information and impartation straight from God. There's no in-between. You are the only one that gets between the Holy Spirit Jesus, and God and stops the Word spoken by way of the Holy Spirit from getting to you. This prevents the evidence of tongues from being seen. This prevents the impartation and information from being present in your life.

People can't see the works that Jesus and the Father do through you if you are in between the Holy Spirit, and not allowing him to work in and through you. This is his job to do what Jesus said. His purpose from God is for you: which is to obey God's commandments and serve God and Him only. Job 36:11 Ish 1:19.

Then ALL your prosperity and promises shall come to past and shall last. You don't want to keep receiving the little; you want the whole lump sum. So you add it ALL up; you choose. You have free will to do so. God also tells you what not to choose, in case you don't know.

This day I call the heavens and the earth as witnesses against you that I have set before you life and death, blessings and curses. Now choose life, so that you and your children may live.

Deuteronomy 30:19 NIV
John 14:12-21, 23-26, 31 KJV
Proverbs 7:1-5, 7-11, 13, 15-19, 21-27 KJV
Proverbs 6:20-33 NIV

August 25@3:22 PM

Unwind and dine, it's harvest time. We have received a whirlwind of blessings that has caught us up and released us into our wealthy place. You have won the race; all because you got in. You were destined to win.

Faith is always about never giving up on the things you believe in God for. God has opened the door. It seems as if you have been here before. This large place fits. I will never quit.

The hunter catches his game when he hunts. Just like the sower receives his harvest when he sows. The seed sown in good soil has no choice but to grow. People of God must continue to sow, sow, and sow. Your gift is in the seed, which always meet the need.

I call today your birthday. God has allowed your money to be birthed today! This is the day that God has made. Receive everything that you prayed. It's His will and pleasure to prosper you. In all that you do continue to say thank you and do what He says to do.

You have your birthrights. This linage began many years before you were born. You have the full ear in the corn. The harvest has come. You never gave up. You kept the pace and stayed in the race. This race that wasn't given to the swift or strong, but to you who have endured unto the end. Enjoy!!!

August 27@9:21 PM

I'm a fighter; I never give up. I can't lose with what the Holy Spirit God gave me to use. When I take a hit; I don't quit. There's no giving up, even though things get tough.

These light afflictions only last for a moment. My moment is up. Yes, it was rough. I obeyed and served. This is the direction and road I chose, as God commanded me. It's everything God promised it would be.

This path is brighter. The load is lighter, because I'm a fighter. I never lose, because of what God gave me to use. I'm equipped; never to be whipped. These signs shall follow me, for all the world to see.

Testimonies have been birthed right here on earth. Obedience has allowed me to hear the promised Spirit of truth. That has come. The evidence is in the tongues. I'm speaking my God ordained, divinely directed decrees for me and the world to see.

My Spirit is pursuing God like never before. I've entered into my place of restoration, rest, revelations, and receiving like never before. On the enemy, I've shut the door. Closed. Do not enter.

What I've spoken from Holy Spirit has come and shall continue to come to pass. It's forever mine. It's always on time. I'm walking in God's divine dominion and destiny. I receive!!!

August 31@9:11 PM

Magnify my magnificent, marvelous, almighty God! God you are wonderful and worthy to be worshipped continually! I give my all to you in all I do. I praise you! I got the power! It's reigning revelations and I'm standing in righteousness. The spirit of the Lord is resting on me, for all the world to see. Increase, increase, and increase it's on me!

I'm free! No more debt on me! Supernatural surplus I receive. No more heaviness. The load has been lightened. I'm debt free! I was made for this large place I'm in. I'm comfortable here. I'm supposed to be here. No more lack. Abundance, abundance, abundance — it's on me. I'm here for all the world to see.

The nations will receive from me. I'm speaking and spreading the good news of the gospel. The power of God is mine. I'm in His divine. The workings of miracles are for me. It's personal.

He has risen just for me to be here. I have the power, might, authority, and strength, in Christ Jesus. I'm supernaturally satisfied. My children and grandchildren are blessed, going out and coming in; we win. We are blessed in the cities and in the fields. God is always near. The pursuit is on; the victory is won, because of His Son. Life is great, because I've done it and continue to do for the kingdom's sake. I receive it all.

September 3@3:55 PM

What I put together, no one can separate. The enemy wants to rob, kill, and steal from you. I come that you have life and life more abundantly. I give you many more and more. Enter into the open doors. What I've opened no man can shut. This is all in my plan.

It's not about man. Man will let you down. I will always be around. Even until the end. This world I created. I've given you everything in it. Rest in my promises. Receive my provisions and prosperity. It's all from me.

I'm not a man. I never lie. Be fruitful and multiply. Continue to pursue me like never before. Watch me continue to open doors. There are many locations, but I've given you destinations. Continue to pray, pray, pray. It's all here to stay.

Blessings, blessings, blessings never stop coming to you. It's my will for you. Now you know what to do. Praise, praise, praise. You will be amazed. In awe of my presence. Worship, worship, worship. It's my spirit of truth in you.

You shall do things for me that you have never done before. I shall do things for you that I've never done before. Live life. Enjoy life. Never let anyone or anything deplete or defeat you. You are living under an open heaven. I have allowed the heavens to open up to you. You have heard from my prophets and apostles. Obey, obey, obey. Blessings are here to stay.

Never try to do things your way. Your way never has a good outcome or ending. Remember, I made your beginning and I shall complete your ending. You decide which way you're going to ride — in the inside lanes or the outside lanes. Inside is better than the outside. Choose the inside lanes.

You have your free will, but I've given you my will. My will is what's best for you. Make sure you do everything I say to do. I shall continue to do a work in you as you do a work in Christ Jesus. Use what you've got.

Power and riches and wisdom and strength and honor and glory and blessings. Remember, the and is for the connection of them all together. You can't have one without the other. I gave them to you this way for you to know that connections are important. Never disconnect with who I told you to connect to. Never connect to who I didn't tell you to connect to.

There are blessings in the right connections, and curses in the wrong connections. Rejoice and be exceedingly glad. In everything rejoice and receive.

September 3@5:15 AM

My soul does openly to the things of the enemy. Satan can't deceive me when I'm hearing, listening, and obeying the Holy Spirit. The spirit of truth is in me. The power of God is resting on me. I'm never defeated and my work is always completed. I'm never competing. I compliment and correct with compassion and confidence in who I am and who's I am — a child of the most high God.

I'm rendering services unto God and reaping the supernatural from God. The enemy is defeated because of what I needed. You need to be saved but do you want to be saved? I'm chosen for a reason — to compel souls to come into this season. Jesus is the reason our sins are forgiven.

Never reach back and get what you've been delivered from. You can't go forward while looking back. Press in and on because the victory is won because of God's Son. We are heirs and joint heirs in Christ Jesus made in His image. We look like Him, do like Him, obey His Father who is our Father.

We cry and call out to Him as we continue to stand peace, promises, and prosperity. It's in our hands. Faith doesn't come with conditions and positions; it comes by believing and hearing God through the Holy Spirit. Heaven is our example.

Make heaven your mentor and you will see things you have never seen before. Shut up and sit down. You are in place. Sometimes, silence is necessary for the suddenly sound to be heard — the sound of a rushing mighty wind to bring deliverance from the sin you got in.

Being filled with the Holy Spirit brings leaping and latching onto the things of God and never letting them depart. Now stand up, stretch out, and start your race. Never allow anything or anyone to cause you to fall on your face. You have crossed the line; it's finished time. You are dining in my divine. Enjoy!

September 10@11:00 AM

God has given us a new heart for each other. We are up on the inside of each other's hearts. Our hearts are open to love and have compassion for each other. There's trust for each other and truths told to each other.

Wrong is recognized and revealed. Right, Wisdom and God's Word is obeyed and received. Our hearts are clean and clear of clog, confusion, and corruption, and continue in correction.

No other male or female can interrupt our hearts for each other. Everything not from God has been evicted from our hearts. God is always in our hearts. The spirit of truth resides in our heart. The Holy Spirit helps us to always recognize the power of God. It rests, rules, resonates, reigns and remains in our hearts forever.

We always believe and receive what God sees, says, and speaks to our hearts. We never receive anything or anyone into our hearts that

God didn't give us. Love is spread abroad in our hearts and it will never depart because we are set apart.

September 12@12:18 AM

There's a sudden turnaround now. Blessing blockers and barriers are removed. You have a burning bush experience. This bush has to be trimmed; otherwise it will grow out of control. Keep your bush trimmed with the Word of God.

You control what you want in life. You choose. Are you going to have order or chaos? Are you going to have things growing wild and out of control? Are you going to let your bush die with no sign of life? Nurture your bush with nutrients; which is everything needed for it to grow and stay trimmed. Make sure your bush is on fire for the Lord and never burn with things that could kill it.

Never neglect to nurture your bush. You are the only one that can take care of your bush. You are responsible for your own bush. Never let anyone or anything put their hands on your bush or destroy the necessary nutrients and things needed for it to live. No one can nurture your bush like you can.

This bush has been divinely given to you. It's planted in the front of your house for all to see, never to be hidden.

Your hands are anointed to prosper and bring fulfillment in every area of your life. Receive from the burning bush experience and know that even though the bush continues to burn, it never burned out. What you do for God should never cease to continue allowing Him to do a work in you. If you allow Him to do the work, then you can work the work He's called you to.

Work the work while it's day, because when the end comes, no one can work. God shall complete this work, so don't stop Him from working the work in you.

Enjoy your payday, which has come. Jesus paid it all for you to receive your call. This bush was chosen as you were chosen to be in the front, flourishing, flowing and being faithful to the maker. "And Moses said, I will now turn aside and see this great sight, why the bush is not burned." Exodus 3:3 AMP

September 13@12:30 AM

I'm blessed, healed, delivered, and set free. The Spirit of the Lord is upon me. The power of God is resting on me. I have what I see, say, and speak. God has done a work in me. I have written the vision, it's plain for all to see, and it speaks — it never lies.

This is the appointed time. Things are unwinding. I'm living in God's divine. It's my time. Seasons come and go. My blessings continue to flow. My marriage is blessed. My ministry and money is blessed. My children and grandchildren are living in the best. They receive more blessings than the rest. They are blessed beyond measure.

The supernatural surplus is here. I'm receiving everything far and everything near: because of what I hear. I listen and I do everything God says to do. I'm living in my best seven years ever. Nothing can stop the overflow because I've begun to grow. Growth comes from planting in the soil, and watering the seed.

I'm receiving from seeds I have sown and seeds unknown. I'm reaping where I have not sown. I'm reaping from seeds people have sown for me. Everything is what God wants it to be in my life. My life is a model for all the world to see.

The spirit of the Lord is upon me. I teach and I reach, because the power of God is resting on me. The kingdom of God is multiplying now. The enemy has been evicted now. No turning back. God change has come because the victory has already been won only because of God's Son. I receive my miracles now.

September 13@1:30 AM

Set, Solid, Stationed, Secure! I've set you here for such a time as this. I'm your solid rock. There's no breaking or bending in you, as you do as I say to do. Obedience is my will for you. You must will to do my will. You have been stationed in this particular place for specific reasons. Stay and pray everyday. There's no other way. You are secure in all you do; I've protected you.

Nothing can come against you that I've not already made a way out for you. Stay in the safety zone. I shall take you places unknown. Rest in me. Let me rule, reign and remain in you. Receive what I've released to you. These breakthroughs in every area of your life are all about what I promised you.

Never fear. I'm always near. I'm never far from you. The ball is in your court. There's no out of bounds. Always inbounds because I'm continually around. You will never be knocked to the ground.

I allowed you to get in the game. You are on the winning team, and controlling the plays. You win, in every play executed. But you must execute the plays. Stick with the plays. Don't deviate from the executed plans and plays. This will cause you to lose the game.

I placed you here to win, make it to your destinations that are designed, destined, and delivered to you. You don't have to look any further. Just expect the great from the great I Am. I Am who I say I Am. I have done what I said I Am. I will continue to do it, through and for you.

The power and blessings of the Lord are on you. Continue in prayer, praise, prophetic, and obedience because this is my will for you.

September 14@2:00 AM

Are you ready to receive? Check the place; see who's in your space. Where you are going, no one can enter in accept they are sent by me, in Jesus' name. You will never be the same.

My Word shall never change. You have full range. The bullets of blessings have been released. There's no knowledge of how fast they are coming. Just know that it's quickly and suddenly, as in the upper room, they have no zoom. They are coming from everywhere. Make sure you are there.

This large place I've set and secured for you. Continue in my Word; that's what you shall do. Pray without ceasing. It's the key. Always praise me. Worship me with all your mind, heart, and soul. You will receive things untold. These blessings I've caused to unfold. Receive them, these are your manifold.

Power, and riches, and wisdom, and strength, and honour, and glory, and blessing. All these, they are connected with the Holy Spirit and Jesus and Me, as you are connected to your almighty, all-powerful God. Know that these blessing didn't come without a price. I've allowed my Son, Jesus, to pay the price for you.

Make sure you continue to be in obedience and do what I say to do. I will continue to make all things come to you. These are things that eyes have not seen nor ears heard. These are things that the Holy Spirit shall reveal to you. Continue to pray in your prayer language because it's the language I've given you by way of the Spirit of Truth.

My Word in John 16:13, it says: Howbeit when he, the Spirit of truth, is come, he will guide you into all truth: for he shall not speak of himself; but whatsoever he shall hear, that shall he speak: and he will shew you things to come.

This I've also spoken to you in John 4:24: God is a Spirit: and they that worship him must worship him in spirit and in truth.

Make sure you keep these two scriptures and live your life by them. Your life depends on them. They are key to hearing from me. Make sure you aren't just a hearer but also a doer.

Again, obedience is key, in being a servant and being served. I will cause men to serve you as you serve me. They shall give unto your bosom. You are my servant. I've called you out to serve.

Again, are your ready to receive? Yes you are.

Always remember to hear from the Holy Spirit, because I'm a Spirit. They that worship me shall do it in spirit and in truth, which is the Spirit of Truth I sent you, and has come to show and teach you all things from me.

Allow him to remind, recall, remain and help you receive all that I've preserved and promoted you for. All that's provided, promised, and shall continue to bring prosperity to you. Enjoy!!!

September 15@10:02 PM

You must be totally sold out to God in obedience to Him in everything you do, even with the things that you think not important to you. The greater the anointing, the greater the trials, tests, temptations and troubles. Why? Because you won't appreciate the triumphs and terrific times that have been predestined and promised to you to prosper.

Everyone can't go where you are going. You will lose friends and even family associations. Everyone can't handle what's been set in order for you. There will be envious people, jealousy and even haters, all because of your greatness and gifts.

The anointing breaks the yokes. The power shuts down and destroys the enemy's power. Greater levels; greater devils. Greater power; greater problems. You must be unreachable to the enemy, much higher than satan's followers — in the Spirit realm.

In these times, you must see the Lord and be high and lifted up. You've got the power and presence of God. He's never far. Question? Will you always recognize and receive Him close? Protect your heart, both what comes in and what goes out. Never let anyone in and anything out that God hasn't divinely given the directives on.

Know God's place, the Holy Spirit's place, your place and the enemy's place. Know that the enemy has no place. Hearing, listening, and obeying are the master keys that unlock the master's blessings, which are manifested and manifold.

Power, riches, wisdom, strength, honour, glory and blessing — again these seven are connected, as connections are powerful. Agreement and speaking the same language. Nothing will be withheld, and nothing that you imagine that God won't do. It's all divinely designed just for you. This is the answer to your question.

You are made for to multiply and not subtract. You shall never turn back. Continue to press toward the mark of the prize of the higher calling, which is in Christ Jesus. As Jesus is, so are you. You have a higher calling.

Your harvest is bigger than most, therefore you have to do and go through more. Endurance to the end. Your ending is your beginning. Notice the word end starts with endurance.

You have dominion in the beginning and dominion in the ending. You must want and will to obey and not do things your way. Before the good comes, there must be obedience. Before the days of prosperity and years of pleasure come, there must be obedience. Choose to obey. You will have what you say.

If ye be willing and obedient, ye shall eat the good of the land, Isaiah 1:19 KJV

If they obey and serve him, they shall spend their days in prosperity, and their years in pleasures, Job 36:11 KJV

But be ye doers of the word, and not hearers only, deceiving your own selves, James 1:22 KJV

Saying with a loud voice, Worthy is the Lamb that was slain to receive power, and riches, and wisdom, and strength, and honour, and glory, and blessing, Revelation 5:12

In the year that king Uzziah died I saw also the Lord sitting upon a throne, high and lifted up, and His train filled the temple, Isaiah 6:1 KJV

I press toward the mark for the prize of the high calling of God in Christ Jesus, Philippians 3:14 KJV

And God blessed them, and God said unto them, Be fruitful, and multiply, and replenish the earth, and subdue it: and have dominion over the fish of the sea, and over the fowl of the air, and over every living thing that moveth upon the earth, Genesis 1:28 KJV

September 19@9:34 AM

Power is flowing through you. Never give up on what I told you to do. My power is in and flowing through you. Again, you got the power. The enemy wants to take it from you. You know what to do. Keep praising and worshiping me; it's the releasing.

Releasing in this spiritual atmosphere. The spirit of truth is in you. Never let up. Never give up. This is how your power will sustain. This is how my power shall continue to reign, remain, rest, rule, remove, replace, and release all things to and from you.

You are my chosen vessel. I chose you in particular for such a time as this. Proceed to check out. Your blessings are released. Check out is where you receive from me. No need to pay. The price has already been paid, because of how you have been made.

You were made to have dominion. Be fruitful, multiply, replenish, and subdue. All these things I have already given you. Rejoice, and be exceedingly glad. The joy of the lord is your strength. You are strong in me, your almighty, all-powerful God.

What I start I always finish. I shall continue to do a work in you. It's my will being done. The victory has already been won, because of the finished work of my Son, in Christ Jesus. You must continue to abide in me and my Words abide in you, and all that you ask according to my will I shall give it to you. This is what I do.

You have my wisdom. You walk in my wisdom. My ways. My Word. My Wealth. Enjoy, it's my pleasure!!!

September 21@3:51 AM

Mediate on your creative ideas and witty inventions. I shall put the thoughts in your mind. It's your time to shine in my divine, for all will see it's all about me. Your almighty, all-powerful God.

Continue to love and pursue me like never before and watch me open doors. Put your money where your mouth is. Remember money is in your mouth and it has to be spoken out.

Giving is loving. Love to give because of your love for me. After all, I gave you the love of my life and now he's the love of your life, my Son, Jesus. Follow My love plan. For I God, so loved the world that I gave my only begotten Son. You are my beloved ones. I loved you even before you were born. Follow after me. This love plan you must follow through as the Holy Spirit speaks to and through you. He will tell you what to do.

Obey my commands in this love plan. You shall love me with all your heart, soul, mind, and might. These are key components. When you love Me, I'm in your heart, soul and mind, as you have the strength and power to hear, listen, and do everything I've chosen, commissioned, and commanded you to do.

Follow my instructions and you shall work the process and receive progress and possessions from me because it pleases me to prosper you in all you do. You shall receive because your motivation comes from loving me. You are blessed far greater than the rest.

Your business shall prosper because you are anointed to prosper. You have great work to do for the kingdom's sake, that's why I've made your name great. People will know who UPE Designs is, because it's all in my will. I'm a man of my Word. What I've spoken shall come to pass, and will always last. You have my Word on it.

The seed you have sown will bring blessings unknown. You have come into your own. The kingdom is in need, that's why I've blessed you indeed. I've enlarged your territory. My hand is on you. No evil can harm you. You are blessed in deed. It's all released because you asked of me and what you asked of me I give because it's according to my will that it's being done in your life. I've worked it all out. Watch me do a work in you, because of what you do.

You have sought the kingdom first and my righteousness, NOW I have added everything unto you. Continue to sow, grow, and flow as I flood and flourish your finances. My prophets have spoken. You have believed them, now you shall receive all that has been spoken.

Again, I say money is in your mouth. It has to be spoken out. Money cometh to me NOW! I've given my Son; therefore the debt has been paid. Money, I gave and it's always ready to be made.

UPE Designs has made you rich and wealthy. You have many venues to receive your revenue. Use them all. I've made your name great. Customers have found you. Get ready to receive extra large orders, quickly and suddenly.

Again, I've set you in this large place. You are a God-made miracle millionaire. Always do what I have told you and shall continue to show you. Keep praying in the Holy Spirit, as my spirit of truth tells you and shows you what to do. Money shall keep on coming to you. Enjoy!!!

September 27@5:22 PM

When we love God and keep His commandments, which is doing what He says, He will not only manifest Himself, but He will protect you before, in, through, and coming out of the storm. You will have confidence in the storm and know that you don't have to run from it because the storm will recognize you and go the other way — as long as you hear, listen, and obey. Always do things Gods way.

God will show you which storms to ride out, and which ones to pack up and leave. The storms you must leave are types of storms that will kill you, so you must leave; you can't stay. Depend on God to show you the way.

When you're traveling down the dark roads of life and things try to turn you upside down; don't fear. Stay calm and in control, because God gave you the wheel. Turn in the direction He wants you to go and everything will immediately get back on track.

When your spouse misunderstands, stays silent, or maybe confused, try communicating with him. If he goes off in another direction, leave him alone; go back to what you were doing. Continue preparing for the storm with confidence, knowing if you should pack up, or stay and ride it out.

Know that you can be preparing for the storm while in the storm, going through the storm and coming out of the storm at the same time. The storms that you are preparing and packing up for are the ones that God says you must leave. The storms that you are in, you are going through and coming out of them.

Know that every time you do good, evil is always present. You must have confidence in knowing that God will allow you to go through just to bring you out. You must speak out your mouth the testimonies of how He brought you out. The best witness is the one who was there when the incident happened. You know first hand what God can do, because He has done it for you. You can witness to others that He will do the same thing for them.

When storms come, always be prepared, have confidence, know your storm, and see if you should ride it out or pack up and leave. When you continue in God's love, while keeping His commandments, and obeying Him, then you can be preparing for a storm while in a storm, going through a storm, and making the right moves with confidence, being fearless, in control, and turning in the right direction. God will set your vehicle and your heart towards Him, which is the direction He has already set up for you. This is the will and Word of God!

September 28@9:32 PM

Simmering slowly, saturated, satisfied, supernaturally soaked in the Word of God. Take your time don't rush through; know who you are giving your service to. The intake of God's Word is a slow process. The ingredients must be settled in good to receive the best taste. Oh, taste and see that God is good. If not simmered slowly or properly, you won't be satisfied with the taste. If not saturated supernaturally soaked, the meat won't be cooked properly, and will be left undone.

Never cease to properly intake of God's Word. Obey and continue slowly for proper and thoroughly following through of His Word, and nothing will be left undone.

We must praise God by speaking to ourselves in Psalms and hymns and Spiritual songs, making melodies in our hearts as unto the Lord. Giving thanks always to the Father, our Lord and saviour, Jesus Christ.

Guard your ear gate, heart and eyes. You can't listen to the world's songs and expect to receive inspiration, impartation, and instructions from God. Music is important. Pay attention to what you hear because God is near in the right atmosphere. You can't worship God with the world's songs because there's no Spirit and truth.

Do what God says to do, and praise your way though. Praise is important. Worship is important. God will speak in these two. The world speaks through their music to you.

Build up your Spirit with the Spirit of truth. The world makes money from there music. God gives you revelations in praise and worship songs, as the melody is made in your hearts as unto Him.

Continue to speak to yourselves in Psalms, hymns and Spiritual songs because this is praise and thanks to God. This is what God expect you to do.

Never give attention to the enemy; this is what he wants you to do. Again, know what you're listening to. Make sure it's building you up and it's desirable and pleasing to God. This makes the enemy seek another heart and home to reside in. You're not hearing what the world is saying through their music, but what God is speaking through His music.

Again, music is important. Remember what God says in His Word.

Singing psalms and hymns and spiritual songs among yourselves, and making music to the Lord in your hearts. And give thanks for everything to God the Father in the name of our Lord Jesus Christ, Ephesians 5:19-20 NLT

October 8@6:00 AM
Tithes and trust. Don't be tight and tip.

Trust God with your tithes and giving. He will show and give you the best in living. Don't tip God. Trust Him. He shall bring it all to pass. God rebukes the devourer for you. Give Him what's due. Watch Him open up the windows of heaven for you.

Try and test God. He will not only give outpouring of blessings, but He will cause the nations to help you with your confessing. The nations shall call you blessed. They shall speak what God has released. You are put to the test, as God himself allows you to test Him and He does the rest.

You are constantly Blessed, a blessing, and made to bless. God made it this way. Continue to follow His lead and sow the seeds. When you can be trusted with very little then you can also be trusted with very much. If you are dishonest with very little, you will also be dishonest with very much. So if you have not been trustworthy in handling worldly wealth, then you will not be trusted with true riches. And if you have not been trustworthy with someone else's property, you will not be given property to own.

God says, don't justify yourselves in the eyes of others, by saying God knows my heart. The things people value highly are detestable in God's sight. Don't break your Covenant with God by withholding tithes. Repent and obey God. Trust Him with your tithes, don't be tight and tip Him. Give your whole tithes and offerings. God doesn't bless the tips, but he does the tithes. Be cheerful givers and watch God provide. Don't just go along for the ride.

You shall receive your prosperity in abundance, all sufficiency, always abounding in every good work. Every good and perfect gift and reward comes from God. When you obey and serve, be willing and obedient, you can decree and declare and God will always be right there. Wherever your there is. God is never far from you when you do as He says do. He has allowed all prosperity to come to you. Enjoy!!!

October 8@8:46 AM

Believe the prophet. Believe what God speaks through him for you. If he says stay where you are right now, believe him, and then God will increase you right where you are. Don't do what you think or feel is right, just because you want it now. God will increase you right where you are now, because you obeyed Him and you believe the prophet so shall you prosper.

The prophet has prayed to God for you that He will show you what to do and where to go. If you obey God, things will work out for you. If you don't obey, things won't work out for you. In your darkest days, light is still continuing to shine. When there was no light I spoke light, and I'm still speaking light today and forever more.

The real prophets have spoken. Believe them because I sent them. If one of my prophets hadn't asked you to come and you came, then you wouldn't have heard the word spoken from one of my other prophets. The first prophet says stay until God releases you and tells you what to do and where to go.

The second prophet says come hear the prophet. The third prophet says someone will say to you and know that you are the one God has chosen to pastor the church. Again, believe the prophets, so shall you prosper.

Don't move until God says move. The move that God says to make will be far greater than the move you would have made. Your moving is coming soon, quickly and suddenly.

Make room. God has set you in this large place. The property is yours for the asking according to God's will. Your big dreams have been fulfilled. It's all for the kingdom's sake and your sake. Know that God makes no mistakes.

Apostle Dr. Leroy Thompson spoke, you are moving now. You received. You must love God like never before. Pursue him like never before. Be thirsty for Him. Seek after Him first. Live in righteousness and all things shall be added unto you.

When you are filled with righteousness, then divine rights become yours. Be careful with what you think and what you say, because you will have it good or bad. You choose. Delight yourself in Him. He shall give you the desires of your heart.

October 10@12:05 PM

I'M HIS
Has spoken
Is speaking
Shall speak

These are reasons why I'm HIS. I have faith and believe that God Has Spoken. Is speaking. Shall speak. I will and want to do all that God says to do. I've made up in my mind that I will obey God at all times. I understand these three key things about life.

1) Righteous Has brought Chastisement
2) Repent Is being Change
3) Receive Shall bring Correction

In order to hear, listen, and do, we must be and stay focused in faith and always do what God says to do. We must choose to live for God by obeying, keeping His commandments, and loving Him. We don't just obey God because we want something from Him or want Him to do something for us. We must live righteous lives at all times.

Know that the chastisement of peace was upon Him, and by His strips we were healed. It's already done, because of God's son, Christ Jesus. He's the reason why we should repent and stay changed, and receive correction.

God has given me the rhythm, the beat, and I'm listening to the sound, as God is always around. God's mind is full of me, and the Spirit of Truth is in me. Look around; see what's there. Oh, taste and see that the Lord is good. Blessed is the man that trusts in Him.

Look behind the things and pay attention to see what's there. Thank God for His bountiful blessings. The atmosphere is right. Continue to pursue and love God like never before. Watch Him continue to open doors, and shut doors He didn't open. Never try and make your wrongs right; this is never pleasing in Gods sight. Just live right.

Whatever your battle is, know that it belongs to the Lord. Keep the faith, and keep obeying. Soon these light afflictions will go away. Keep praying, praising, and worshipping. Remember God is a Spirit and they that worship Him must do so in Spirit and in truth, and again know that you have the Spirit of truth in you.

You never loose with the equipment God gave you to use. He has equipped His saints, the set apart ones He's called to serve. God gives you the desires of your heart and they must line up with what He desires for you. Things you deserve and didn't deserve. God's grace and mercy is yours. Enjoy!

October 27@3:32 AM
I got the Feeling!

He's indwelling in me. I love this feeling abiding on the inside. This is where God abides. I'm letting go and taking this ride in stride. I got the power — power that destroys all my enemies. God gave me this authority, might, ability, and strength.

Some were called and others went. Oh, thank God for choosing me. I'm called for this purpose, which is to build up not torn down. God shall always be around. He's never far, and He has set me apart. The enemy has to depart.

I'm up on the inside of Gods heart. My thoughts are His thoughts. My ways are His ways. I shall always do what He says. Obedience, I'm in line, and it's my time. I receive. I believe. It's all laid up for me. The wealth of the wicked is mine. I'm living in God's divine.

I'm declaring and decreeing things. I love my almighty God with all my heart, mind, might, and soul. I'm receiving blessings untold. I don't know how, they are just untold and about to unfold. These manifestations I behold. They were all set up before time. They are God's divine.

Again, it's my time. Blessings are about to unwind. The whirlwind is whistling. The horn is blowing. The trumpet is sounding. Increase is here. Prophets have spoken. Prophets have prayed and hands they have laid.

I see the light in the shade. I got it made. No darkness. This is a continual shinning and brightness of light, never to burn out. I'm out. I'm out. This I shout. Hallelujah! Hallelujah! Hallelujah! Jesus! Jesus! Jesus! These are my three: My father, His son, and His Holy Spirit. The fourth, His angels. I never discount or discredit His angels working, ministering, protecting, and bringing prosperity.

The curse is broken off my husband, my family, and all that concern me. I'm blessed in the cities. I'm blessed in the fields. The harvest is here. The crops have come up in abundance. The bands and chains are loosed. I'm free of everything that was holding me. No more lack. No more being in want. No more debt. Supernatural surplus and no more sickness.

I'm the healed, delivered, blessed, and a set free woman of God. My life, God has turned it around for me. He has blessed me indeed.

He has enlarged my territory. His hand is with me. The blessings shall always be with me.

I'm rejoicing. I'm exceedingly glad. I have more money than I've ever had. Thank you Lord! I receive! I receive! I receive!

November 1@2:05 PM

I'm all in. I always win. I'm a baller. I'm getting taller. I never fail. I never cause my gift to be derailed. I have been given the gift. I never let anyone's demands destroy it. I live right. I just do it.

God is looking for His people he's called out to get His Word out. The kingdom is in need and God has blessed me indeed. He has enlarged our coasts. We must love God the most. Love Him with all our heart, mind, and soul. By Grace we have received it all through faith.

Know that grace and faith cannot work without each other. I have come from the rear. My time is here. I have exploded. I'm on the road. Many stops. Plenty of things to drop. Plenty of deposits, and plenty of withdrawals. God's Word deposits, and the Holy Spirit withdraws.

Your journey has begun. You have already won. Nothing can stop you. You know what to do. You are more than a conqueror. You are a victor not a victim. You are released into increase. You are not living in just enough; you are living in more than enough. It's on you. It's in you. It's coming through you. It's what I want to do. It's my pleasure to prosper you.

Raise your hands, as people began to stand. They are standing for right and righteousness. You are more powerful than the rest. You are my very best. Sickness and disease is canceled and cursed from the root. Lack and being in want is gone. There are no roots to come up again. Ashes to ashes, dust to dust, they're all dead.

The anointing and oil is in your hands. Raise your hands, and again I say stand. You shall lay hands on the sick and they shall recover. Money shall keep on coming to you. It's for the great work I have for you to do. Follow through.

You have written the vision. It's plain for all to see. Money, it's always in your mouth. It has to be spoken out. Money cometh to me

NOW! Wow, so much money coming to me NOW! You are covered. No pimps. No pressure. You never lose, with what I allow my Spirit to speak through you. Speak, speak, speak.

Harvest, harvest, harvest. The crops have come up. Plenty, plenty, plenty. You got this. Never get weary in well doing. You have reaped. There's no fainting in you. Remember my Word in Galatians 2:20: My old self has been crucified with Christ. It is no longer I who live, but Christ lives in me. So, I live in this earthly body by trusting in the Son of God, who loved me and gave himself for me. The strength is in the two that I put together.

Don't let anything or anyone separate you. Know that what I joined together stays together. Agreement and speaking the same language is the key. It's all about me. Hear this Word, because it's straight from my mouth. I've brought you out and into all these blessings that's on you NOW!

People have been waiting on you. It's time to walk in my divine. You are delivered, dominating, and designated to make it to your destinations. Work and walk out this work I'm working in you. It's my will being done. The victory has already been won because of my beloved son, Christ Jesus, that's the reason.

November 7@10:35 AM

The power of God is resting in you. You are about to see what your all mighty, all-powerful God has done for you. He's done it for Apostle Leroy Thompson. He's done it for you.

The money cometh anointing is on him and on you. He's a money magnet and so are you. The heavens are wide open. Now, receive all your blessings that have been stolen from you. They were preserved and waiting on you to serve. You are His servant, called, chosen, and commissioned to serve.

You are holy as He is holy, with no strings attached, and unconditional love for God. You shall go very far and very fast. Your victories will last. You will never go back into your past. Stay away from those that try and take you there, even your family, which you like communicating with. Evil communication corrupts good manners, even if you think it's not harmful, it is.

What come from the mouth reaches the heart. Keep it clean. You know what I mean. I'm allowing your light to shine. It's all in my divine. You are destined for dominion. Walk in it. Every place where the soles of your feet shall tread upon is yours. So start threading. You are all in.

Walk in the lanes that are wide open for you. You have my permission. It's my pleasure to prosper and position you in this large place. Rejoice and be exceedingly glad again I say rejoice!!!

About the Author

Lady Mary Hatter is a wife, mother, grandmother and Co-Founder of Kingdom Minded Church with her husband, Pastor A.D. Hatter. Lady Mary, her husband, daughter, son and granddaughter reside in Spring, Texas.

Lady Mary is the founder of Gods C.H.A.S.E.D. Women, a women's fellowship that meets every second Saturday of the month. She has an unwavering compassion, along with her faithfulness to build up women in the body of Christ and the in world. She teaches them to become great wives, mothers, and to live single with God; learn to control their tongues, and finally to love themselves and others; in spite of the wrong they have done to themselves and others.

She is anointed to teach the Word of God. God has given her the prophetic anointing to speak His secrets; which are His Word, and to build up the church: His body of baptized believers. Devoted to the vision of the ministry of Kingdom Minded Church, she assists her husband, A.D. Hatter, Pastor and Founder.

Lady Mary received a Literary Award from the Association of Independent Ministries in 2012.

A.R.I.S.E.

Additional
Resources
Information
Special
Events

Website: Maryhatter.com
Twitter: @LadyMaryHatter
Facebook: UPE Deisgns Tsits
Business: 281.254.5994

Also available as an ebook from
Amazon.com, BarnesandNoble.com, iBooks and other ebook retailers

*Surely the Lord God will do nothing,
but he revealeth his secret unto his servants the prophets.*
~Amos 3:7:

www.ingramcontent.com/pod-product-compliance
Lightning Source LLC
Chambersburg PA
CBHW052020070526
44584CB00016B/1832